SCIENTIFIC AMERICAN

Great Science Fair Projects

Scientific American
and
Marc Alan Rosner

Illustrated by Cheryl Kirk Noll

John Wiley & Sons, Inc.

New York • Chichester • Weinheim • Brisbane • Singapore • Toronto

. . . .

To Christine, who wrote with me, and Keira,
the youngest Amateur Scientist.

The publisher and the author have made every reasonable effort to ensure that the experiments
and activities in the book are safe when conducted as instructed but assume no responsibility for
any damage caused or sustained while performing the experiments or activities in this book.
Parents, guardians, and/or teachers should supervise young readers who undertake the experiments and activities in this book.

ISBN: 0-471-35625-5

Contents

Physics 81

Introduction

The editors of *Scientific American* magazine have been linking scientists and showing new scientific developments since 1845. Now with this book, they'd like to share some of their experiments with you. If you're reading this book, you also must have some interest in practical science. Perhaps you have a science fair exhibit to design. Or a class assignment. Or simply an interest in conducting science and learning things on your own. Whatever your reasons, there has never been a more exciting time to become an Amateur Scientist.

Science Research Resources

There are many places you can research science:

1. Your school science department and library
2. Your local public library
3. Bookstores
4. Science suppliers
5. The Internet

The Internet is a special place for science research. It was invented by scientists to share information. Here are just a few web sites with general science information that you may find useful.

Science Equipment Suppliers

Arbor Scientific:
 www.arborsci.com/
Carolina Biological:
 www.carosci.com/
Edmund Scientific:
 www.edsci.com/

General Science Project and Fair Sites

Dr. Internet's Science Projects:
 www.ipl.org/youth/DrInternet/
 experiment.main.html

The Exploratorium:
 www.exploratorium.edu/
OMSI Science Learning Network:
 www.omsi.edu/sln/
Science Hobbyist home page:
 www.eskimo.com/~billb/
Vicki Cobb's Kids' Science Page:
 www.vickicobb.com/
Virtual Science Fair:
 www.parkmaitland.org/sciencefair/
 index.html
The Why Files:
 whyfiles.news.wisc.edu/index.html

"Ask a Scientist" Sites

Ask a Scientist or Engineer:
 www.nsf.gov/nstw_questions/start.htm
Ask an Astronomer:
 imagine.gsfc.nasa.gov/docs/ask_astro/
 ask_an_astronomer.html
Mad Scientist Network:
 www.madsci.org/
NASA Ask a Scientist:
 imagine.gsfc.nasa.gov/poetry//ask/
 askmag.html

Scientific American Family of Sites

Scientific American home page:
 www.sciam.com/
Scientific American Archive:
 www.sciamarchive.com
Scientific American Ask an Expert:
 www.sciam.com/askexpert/
Scientific American Discovering Archaeology:
 www.discoveringarchaeology.com
Scientific American Explorations:
 www.explorations.org/
Scientific American Frontiers:
 www.pbs.org/saf/
Society for Amateur Scientists:
 www.sas.org/

The Scientific Method

Scientific study can take different forms. As an Amateur Scientist, you can study natural phenomena, build models, interpret and explain processes, or interview a practicing scientist. The most formal investigation you can conduct is an **experiment**. In an experiment, the scientist follows the **scientific method**.

> Aristotle (384–322 B.C.), the ancient Greek philosopher, is known as the father of the **scientific method** for his work in natural science.

1. *State the **problem**.* The problem is usually posed as a question. For example, the problem could be, "Why do hydrangeas sometimes turn blue, and sometimes red?"

2. *Form a **hypothesis**.* The **hypothesis** is a possible explanation for the problem. Your goal is to see whether the hypothesis is a suitable explanation. Your hypothesis could be, "Perhaps the acidity of the soil determines hydrangea color."

3. *Test your hypothesis through an **experiment**.* In the testing phase, you gather data under controlled conditions. The experiment in this example would be to grow hydrangeas in two different soil conditions—one acidic, the other basic. As much as possible, you should take careful observations, document your technique; and present your data clearly, using tables, graphs, and diagrams where appropriate.

4. *Draw **conclusions**.* In this final phase of the scientific method, you analyze your experimental findings to evaluate your original hypothesis and answer the question you asked in the first place. For example, "Hydrangeas grow blue in soil treated with acid, and pink in soil treated with base. From this we can conclude that hydrangea color is indeed related to soil acidity."

> In a controlled experiment, the **variable** is the factor you are changing to examine its effects, the **control** is the factor you hold constant, and **data** are your observations, numerical or otherwise.

A Note on Safety

The experiments and activities in this book have been chosen for their practicality and safety. Always observe the following precautions as you conduct science experiments:

- Follow instructions carefully, and get adult assistance where specified or needed.

- Obey all rules of laboratories, libraries, and other facilities where you visit and work.

- Wear safety goggles with side protectors when working with glass, chemicals, or fast-moving objects.

- Do not bring food or drink to the area where you are experimenting.

- Take special care in handling electricity and chemicals.

- Know the location and use of safety equipment, such as fire extinguishers and first-aid kits.

- Report any accidents or problems to an adult.

ASTRONOMY

1 Making a Sundial

Before there were mechanical clocks, people used the Sun to tell time. As Earth rotates about its axis, the Sun appears to be moving through the sky, changing its position—even though it is really we who are spinning. Sundials use the change in the Sun's position to measure time. In the morning, your shadow points long into the west as the sun rises in the east. As noon approaches, your shadow gets shorter. Then your shadow points eastward, increasing again, as the Sun sets. The length of your shadow also depends on your **longitude** (distance east or west of the prime meridian, measured by imaginary lines running from the North Pole to the South Pole). In northern winters, the Sun is low in the southern sky and casts a long shadow through most of the day. This results from the tilt in Earth's axis, which gives us seasons.

> Earth's axis is tilted 23 degrees. **Precession** is the wobbling of Earth's axis over tens of thousands of years. The **eccentricity** of Earth's orbit is its deviation from a perfect circle. (For more on eccentricity, see chapter 4, "Demonstrating Orbits.")

Materials

- tape
- sheet of large paper
- 3-to-4-mm-thick sheet of corrugated cardboard or plywood
- hammer
- long nail
- watch
- marker
- ruler

Procedure

1. Find a sunny location on a clear day. Begin early in the morning.

2. Tape a sheet of paper to the cardboard.

3. Hammer a nail into the center of the paper, just far enough in so that it stands firmly on its own.

> The part of a sundial that casts a shadow is called a **gnomon.**

4. Mark the shadow of the nail at 1-hour intervals (e.g., 8:00 A.M., 9:00 A.M., etc.). Mark the shadow of the head of the nail, then draw the shadow of the nail using a straightedge or ruler. Mark the time of day. *It is very important that you do not change the position of your board during the day.*

5. At the end of the day, you will have a functional sundial! Record the date and location (city, state) on your sundial.

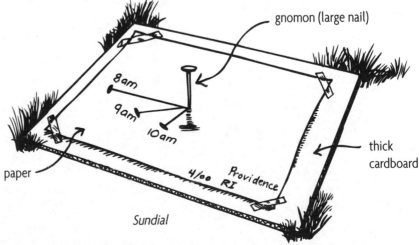

gnomon (large nail)

8am
9am
10am

paper

4/00 RI Providence

thick cardboard

Sundial

> Your sundial is **calibrated** to work in your particular longitude. The farther you travel from where you made your sundial, the less accurate it will be.

6. You can use your paper as a template to make a sundial out of more durable and attractive materials, such as wood, plastic, metal, and so on.

> You have constructed a horizontal-dial sundial. There are other types of sundials—for instance, vertical ones. To make a vertical sundial, mount your paper on an upright board that is perpendicular to the ground, and facing south if you live in the Northern Hemisphere.

7. If you move your sundial, recalibrate it by positioning it to read the proper time. You'll have to recalibrate it twice a year anyway if your region goes on and off of daylight saving time.

8. As an extension to this activity, you can make sundials at different times during the year and compare them. The position of the Sun in the sky and hence the shadow changes with the rotation and revolution of Earth.

> At the ancient monument Chichén Itzá on Mexico's Yucatán Peninsula, a shadowy snake climbs up the steps during the **vernal equinox** (the time in late March each year when the Sun crosses the equator and day and night are equal in length everywhere). The ancient Mayan designers used mathematics and their understanding of astronomy to engineer a structure that would give this effect.

References

Sundials: Their Theory and Construction by Albert Edmund Waugh (Mineola, N.Y.: Dover, 1973).

Making a Clock-Accurate Sundial Customized to Your Location (for the Northern Hemisphere) by Sam Muller (Happy Camp, Calif.: Naturegraph, 1997).

Scientific American exhibit—Mars Sundial: www.sciam.com/exhibit/1999/042699 sundial/index.html

Sundials on the Internet: www.sundials.co.uk/

2 Photographing Lunar Eclipses

There is nothing as beautiful as a **lunar eclipse.** In a lunar eclipse, Earth passes between the Sun and the Moon, casting a shadow on the Moon. As the Moon darkens, it looks as if it is going through its phases, but really it is not. The color of the Moon's surface may change through many hues, including white, yellow, red, and brown. You can get the dates of future lunar eclipses from an almanac or the Internet. Unlike a **solar eclipse,** in which the Moon passes between the Sun and Earth, casting a shadow on Earth, a lunar eclipse may be safely viewed with the naked eye. And you don't need fancy equipment to record images of a lunar eclipse. In fact, a basic camera and astronomy equipment work just fine.

Materials

- almanac or Internet access
- camera
- zoom or telephoto lens, or telescope and adapter (optional)
- high-speed film
- tripod
- notebook and pencil
- cable release (optional)
- video camera (optional)

Procedure

1. Establish the dates of coming lunar eclipses from an almanac or the Internet, and prepare well in advance.
2. Choose your photographic equipment. If possible, use a single-lens reflex (SLR) camera that takes 35-mm film.

You should be able to set the **aperture** or **f-stop** (the size of the opening that lets in light) and the **shutter speed** (the length of time the camera's shutter opens to let in light) manually; however, an automatic shutter or aperture feature is useful to gauge the light levels. If you are not using a telescope, use the most powerful camera lens available to you—a 70-mm zoom or telephoto lens will work better than a 35-mm wide-angle lens. If you are using a telescope, you can get a telescope adapter that will attach your camera to the end of your telescope from Edmund Scientific or another optical/astronomy equipment supplier. If you do this, you will want to use a telescope that has a motor drive, to help track objects accurately and keep them centered in the field of view. You must use high-speed film—ASA 800 or higher. Color film may be easier to process, and will show the reddish brown colors that often accompany lunar eclipses.

3. Load your film, then mount the camera on a tripod or attach it to a telescope that is mounted on a tripod. It's best to practice in advance, during a non-eclipse night, to perfect your photographic technique. Bear in mind that the Moon's position in the sky shifts rather quickly from east to west, so you have to keep checking the camera periodically to be sure it's still aimed in the right direction. When you take pictures, you should record your camera settings in a log for each frame.

35-mm camera

tripod→

4. Open the aperture all the way to let in the maximum amount of light. The lower the number (e.g., 3.5, 1.4 . . .), the wider the aperture.

5. Use a cable release, if available, to trip the shutter without jarring the camera. Use slow shutter speeds to get a good exposure of the Moon's low light. If your camera has an automatic shutter speed feature, it will probably adjust itself to the right setting. But you can also do this manually. Start at the slowest shutter speed (which may be ½ second or longer) and move up to a faster speed (up to, but not much faster than, ⅛ second).

Photographers sometimes use handheld light meters. Light intensity is measured in different units, such as **lumens** and **footcandles**. A footcandle is an old unit of light intensity: 1 footcandle is the amount of light cast by a candle at a distance of 1 foot!

---

6. Even if you don't have a telephoto lens or telescope, when you get your photographs back from processing, you can enlarge the good ones. You will get excellent detail with 35-mm or larger film. If you have access to a photo lab, you can control the printing yourself.

7. Although we won't discuss the use of a video camera here, you can certainly try to use one to videotape a lunar eclipse, using methods based on this discussion. With the right setup, you can import video footage into your computer and make an interactive presentation.

References

The Cambridge Eclipse Photography Guide: How and Where to Observe and Photograph Solar and Lunar Eclipses by Michael A. Covington; Jay M. Pasachoff, ed. (Cambridge, Engl.: Cambridge University Press, 1993).

Eclipse: An Introduction to Total and Partial Eclipses of the Sun and Moon by Ian Bruce (Harrogate, Engl.: Take That, 1999).

Eclipse! The What, Where, When, Why, and How Guide to Watching Solar and Lunar Eclipses by Philip S. Harrington (New York; John Wiley & Sons, 1997).

Astronomy Online lunar eclipse page: www.eso.org/outreach/spec-prog/aol/ market/collaboration/luneclipse/ luneclipse.html

Eclipse home page: Sunearth.gsfc.nasa.gov/eclipse/eclipse.html

Lunar Eclipse Observer home page: www.spirit.net.au/~minnah/leox.html

Sky and Telescope's eclipse page: www.skypub.com/sights/eclipses/ eclipses.html

Tracking Artificial Satellites

Sometimes, when you look into the night sky, you see an object that looks like a star, but it is moving too quickly to be a star and too slowly to be a "shooting star," or **meteor** (a fragment of matter from space that enters Earth's atmosphere and ignites from friction against atmospheric gases). Chances are you are seeing an artificial satellite, made by people and put in Earth's orbit for the purpose of telecommunications or military intelligence. With a simple **astrolabe** (a device for determining the size and position of celestial bodies and other objects in the sky), you can calculate the altitude of the satellite.

> Don't bother trying to view a satellite through a telescope. It moves too fast to be visible through a telescope, and if you do manage to see it, it will simply look brighter. Binoculars are a better choice for viewing moving objects.

Materials

- wood saw
- meterstick
- four 180-cm-long wooden dowels or strips of narrow molding (Use thin, light wood about 10 mm in diameter, similar to the wood used in a meterstick. The lighter, the better.)
- hammer
- 4 roofing nails
- protractor
- paintbrush
- white paint
- flashlight
- stopwatch

Procedure

Build Your Astrolabe

1. Saw a 30-cm length off each of two dowels.

2. Join the two 150-cm dowels you just made side by side by hammering a nail through one end.

3. Spread the dowels 10 degrees apart, using a protractor.

> There are 360 degrees in a circle. Your astrolabe describes an arc equal to one thirty-sixth of the range of the night sky.

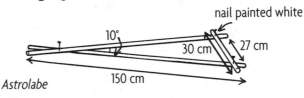

Astrolabe

4. Fasten one of the 30-cm scrap pieces to each of the free ends of the dowels, using two nails to nail it in place. Make sure the nails are hammered in the same direction as the nail in step 2.

5. Paint the three nails white where they protrude from the wood and allow the paint to dry.

6. Join together the two remaining 183-cm dowels with hammer and nail near (20 cm) one end. Swivel the free ends apart about two handbreadths and push them into the soil as shown. This will act as a support for the astrolabe. Place your astrolabe on the supports as shown and position yourself as indicated.

> The **zenith**, or the highest point in the sky, is the best place to find satellites and track their movement.

7. Place a flashlight so that it will illuminate the nails. Use a low-level light— you want enough light to be able to see the nails, but not so much light that you can't see the sky easily.

Make Your Measurements

1. The best time to make measurements is just after sunset or before sunrise on a very clear night.

2. Practice viewing the night sky through the astrolabe. Look along the line of sight from the lower nail to one of the upper nails. Line the nails up with a star. Now look along the line of sight of the second upper nail.

3. When you spot a satellite, swing the astrolabe into position so that the two upper nails are lined up in the path of the approaching satellite.

4. When the satellite passes the first nail, use the stopwatch to start counting the seconds. Stop the stopwatch when the satellite passes the second nail.

> An easy way to count seconds without having to handle the stopwatch is to count "one 1,000, two 1,000," and so on. If you choose this method, practice first to make sure your pace is accurate.

5. Use the Transit Times and Altitudes table to find the altitude of your satellite.

TRANSIT TIMES AND ALTITUDES

10 Degrees transit time (seconds)	Altitude (miles)
2	56
3	84
4	112
5	138
6	166
7	193
8	219
9	246
10	273
12	325
14	375
16	426
18	477
20	526
25	650
30	770
35	890
40	1,000
50	1,225
60	1,450
70	1,660
80	1,860
90	2,060
100	2,250
120	2,620
140	2,980

> As a satellite encounters atoms and molecules of air, it slows down. When the orbital time of a satellite decreases to about 87 minutes, the satellite falls through the lower atmosphere and is consumed in a fireball caused by friction!

References

Planets and Satellites (Window on the Universe) by Robert Estalella and Marcel Socias (Hauppauge, N.Y.: Barron's Juveniles, 1993).

Satellites (20th-Century Inventions series) by Steve Parker (Orlando, Fla.: Raintree/Steck-Vaughn, 1997).

All the planets of our solar system, including Earth, orbit the Sun in elliptical paths. An **ellipse** is a curve generated by a point moving in such a way that the sum of the point's distances from two fixed points on the curve is a constant. You can imagine an ellipse as an oval—a circle that is squashed a bit, as if someone sat on it. In fact, Earth's orbit is nearly circular. In this activity, you will generate orbits and analyze their shapes.

Nicolaus Copernicus (1473–1543) was the first astronomer to propose a Sun-centered or **heliocentric** model of our solar system. Earlier, people believed that Earth was the center of our solar system. Johannes Kepler (1571–1630), a mathematician, was the first to conclude that planetary orbits are elliptical.

Materials

- 2 sheets of white paper
- pencil
- piece of corrugated cardboard (or a bulletin board)
- 2 sturdy pushpins (Dissection pins work well.)
- metric ruler
- 30-cm string with ends joined in loop

Procedure

1. Fold a sheet of paper in half, then unfold it and fold it in half again, this time the other way. Open the paper and mark the point where the two folds cross with the letter *C* (center).

2. Place the paper lengthwise on a piece of cardboard or a bulletin board, and tape it down.

3. Place a pin along the long fold 1 cm from the left of the marked center. Label this pin "Sun." Its position will remain fixed throughout the experiment.

4. Select five points along the long fold at different distances to the right of the center mark and number them 1, 2, 3, 4, and 5. Place the second pin in position 1.

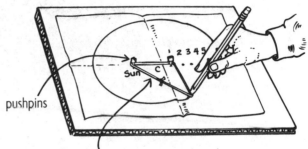

Drawing an ellipse   30-cm string tied in a loop

5. Place the loop of string over both pins. Put the pencil through the loop and pull the string until it's taut. Move the pencil to a 12 o'clock position. Trace an ellipse by moving the pencil all the way around the "clock," keeping the string taut.

Size of planets is exaggerated.

Elliptical planetary orbits

RELATION OF ORBITAL SHAPE TO DISTANCE FROM SUN

Position	Distance between pins (cm)	Orbit 1 (cm)	Orbit 2 (cm)	Orbital shape
1				
2				
3				
4				
5				

6. Measure (in centimeters) and record the following: (a) the distance between the Sun and the second pin, (b) the lengths of the orbit along the long and short folds of the paper (orbits 1 and 2), and (3) the shape of the orbit.

7. Repeat steps 5 and 6, placing the second pin in each of the other four positions you marked in step 4.

8. Record your data in a table like the one shown.

> The Moon's orbit of Earth is fairly eccentric ($e = 0.55$), giving rise to noticeable effects, such as the easily observed changes in apparent size of the Moon and noticeable differences in tides. Comets have highly eccentric orbits. Pluto has such a high eccentricity that astronomers recently debated whether it should even be considered a planet.

9. How did the orbital shape change as the distance between the two pins increased? Predict the shape you'd obtain if you placed the two pins very close together.

References

Janice VanCleave's the Solar System: Mind-Boggling Experiments You Can Turn into Science Fair Projects by Janice VanCleave (New York: John Wiley & Sons, 2000).

Nine Planets:
www.seds.lpl.arizona.edu/billa/tnp/

Raman's Orbital Simulator:
www.explorescience.com/orbit.htm

Views of the Solar System:
www.hawastsoc.org/solar/

> Eccentricity is the deviation of an orbital shape (ellipse) from a perfect circle.
>
> One formula for eccentricity (e) is:
>
> $$e = 1 - \frac{\text{shorter length (called the ellipse's minor axis) of orbit}}{\text{longer length (major axis) of orbit}}$$
>
> You can use this formula to calculate the eccentricity of your ellipses.
>
> When the minor axis equals the major axis (as in the case of a circle), the fraction in the formula equals 1, so the eccentricity equals 0. Earth's eccentricity is small: $e = 0.00167$. When $e = 1$, the geometric figure is a **parabola**, a curve generated by a point moving in such a way that the point's distance from a fixed line is equal to its distance from a fixed point not on the line.

BIOLOGY

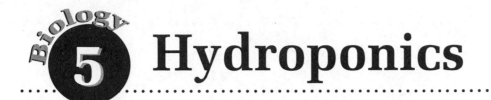

Hydroponics

Hydroponics is the science of growing plants in nutrient solutions rather than in soil. The **nutrients** in these liquids are chemicals that provide energy and promote or stimulate growth and life. In this activity, you compare different growing conditions, such as the ingredients in your nutrient solution, or "broth," and the type of media that your plants are rooted in, such as gravel, sand, and so on, to find out what conditions work best to nurture plants.

> Hydroponics may be the most efficient way to grow vegetables on the Moon or on other planets where there is no soil.

Materials

You can acquire the materials needed for this experiment from aquarium suppliers, garden shops, hardware stores, and hobby shops.

- safety razor (*requires adult help*)
- large plastic container (Rubbermaid dishpan size works well.)
- approximately 2 m of plastic tubing (aquarium tubing or hose) to match pump
- metric ruler
- silicone aquarium or bathroom sealant
- large piece of wire screen
- utility scissors
- lightweight water pump, or second container, tube, clamp, and tray (You can use a pump designed for outdoor fountains and pools, or modify an aquarium pump.)
- wire (may be useful for securing and supporting tubes)
- wire cutters
- plant seeds (Beans and peas work well.)
- assorted root media (e.g., perlite, vermiculite, pumice, gravel, sand, sawdust, peat moss)
- assorted nutrient compounds (magnesium sulfate, calcium phosphate, potassium nitrate, calcium sulfate, potassium chloride)
- meterstick or tape measure
- notebook and pencil
- metric scale
- metric measuring cup
- 1-L (liter) pitcher
- water

Procedure

Build Your Hydroponic Facility.

1. Have an adult use a safety razor to cut a hole close to the bottom of one of the walls of a plastic container. The hole should be the same size as the outside diameter of your tubing so that the tube fits snugly in the hole. Pass the tube through the hole, from the outside, 1 cm into the container. Apply sealant to the area between the tube and the container on both sides, and allow it to harden overnight. Apply more sealant if necessary for a good seal and allow that to dry. Cut a 5-cm-diameter circular piece of wire screen with utility scissors, place it over the inside opening of the tube, and secure it in place with sealant. The screen prevents clogging. Save the rest of the screen for later.

2. Connect the free end of the tube to the water pump intake. Connect a second tube, from the outflow of the pump, back to the top of the container. This is for the return flow. Have an adult make a hole at the top of the container for the return flow tube, and seal it in place as you did the other tube.

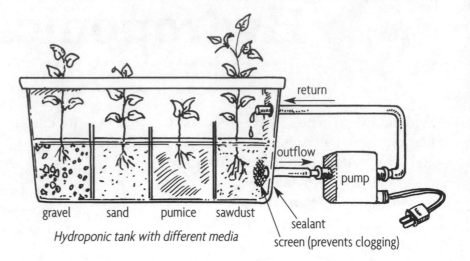

Hydroponic tank with different media

gravel   sand   pumice   sawdust

return

outflow

pump

sealant

screen (prevents clogging)

3. After positioning and attaching the tubes, and waiting for the sealant to dry, check all connections to make sure they are secure. If you feel that the tubes might pull away from the apparatus or lose their seal, you can secure them with wire. Gently twist one end of the wire around itself into a loop on one end of the tube connection. Then wrap the wire around the object to which the tube is connected (e.g., the container). Then cut the wire, leaving enough wire free to fasten it to

the tube again, near the wire loop. Do this for each tube as needed.

Design and Conduct Your Experiment

1. You will place seeds in the medium in the hydroponic container, and circulate nutrient broth to allow them to grow. What you have to decide is:

• What variables will you change?

• How will you measure plant growth?

The main variables you can control are the root media and the nutrient broth. You can measure plant growth with a simple meterstick or tape measure. Record the distance from the soil line

If you can't get a water pump, you can create a drip apparatus with a second container, a tube, and a clamp. The tube runs out of one hydroponic tank (supported on a shelf, ladder, or table) and into the other, like an IV. You regulate the dripping with the clamp, collect the outflow in a tray, and return it to the drip container twice a day.

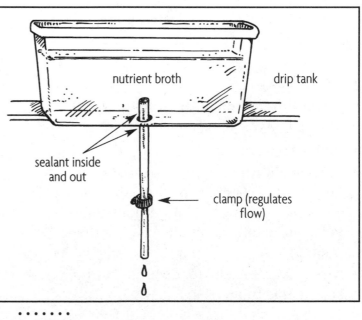

nutrient broth

drip tank

sealant inside and out

clamp (regulates flow)

NUTRIENT COMPOUNDS AND PLANT GROWTH

Trial	Magnesium sulfate	Calcium phosphate	Potassium nitrate	Calcium sulfate	Potassium chloride	Average plant height at 1 week
1	✔	✔	✔	✔		
2	✔	✔	✔		✔	
3	✔	✔		✔	✔	
4	✔		✔	✔	✔	
5		✔	✔	✔	✔	

to the top of the plant, gently extending the plant to its full length.

2. To make nutrient broth, dissolve in water small quantities of different combinations of the nutrient compounds listed in the materials section: 250 to 750 mg/L of water. One idea would be to use four out of five of each of the compounds in five trials, each time leaving out one of the compounds to see which one is most essential. Be sure to use the same amount of each nutrient in each trial.

3. To test different media, you can divide your container into square sections with extra wire screen and use a different media mixture in each section. What conditions work best? For instance, you can determine which two media work best together.

Record the average plant height after a specific time (e.g., 2 weeks) for the

> You can also compare different concentrations of nutrient broth. Make several five-compound mixtures, one containing 250 mg/L of each compound, another containing 500 mg/L, and so on.

gravel-sand mixture, the gravel-pumice mixture, and so on, adding as many combinations in additional columns and rows as you see fit.

References

Beginning Hydroponics: A Beginners Guide to Growing Vegetables, House Plants, Flowers, and Herbs without Soil by Richard E. Nicholls (Philadelphia: Running Press, 1990).

Exploring Classroom Hydroponics (Growing Ideas series) by Eve Pranis and Joreen Hendry (Burlington, Vt.: National Gardening Association, 1995).

Bradley Hydroponics web site: www.hydrogarden.com/az.htm

MEDIA MIXTURES AND PLANT GROWTH

Gravel	Sand	Pumice	Sawdust	Average plant height
✔	✔			
✔		✔		
✔			✔	
	✔	✔		
	✔		✔	
		✔	✔	

6 Stimulation of Plant Growth

When young rice plants are infected with the fungus *Gibberella fujikuroi*, they grow extraordinarily tall. Some 70 years ago, a

> A **fungus** is a group of spore-producing organisms that feed on dead or decaying matter. **Spores** are seedlike reproductive units.

Japanese plant physiologist discovered that an extract of the fungus produced the same effect. Gibberellic acid is now commercially available from garden supply stores. It has remarkable growing effects on plants—a speck smaller than a grain of sugar can spur the growth of an entire window box. This chemical is useful to florists, farmers, researchers, and home gardeners.

> Gibberellic acid, a **hormone** (a chemical substance that stimulates growth or other chemical activity), is sold by nursery supply houses for plant breeding and hybridizing. If you have trouble locating it, you can substitute another chemical sold for the purpose of stimulating growth. Try to find a stimulant with only one active ingredient, rather than a fertilizing blend, in order to study just one variable.

Materials

- 4 packages of pea seeds (same variety)
- water
- paper towels or sawdust
- bowl
- notebook and pencil
- 32 paper drinking cups
- metric ruler
- sifted topsoil or potting soil
- pen and masking tape (for labeling cups and bottles)
- 7 dropper bottles with a capacity of approximately 100 mL (available at drugstores, medical supply stores, or housewares stores. Ideally, they should be marked on the side with cubic centimeters or milliliters.)
- metric balance
- gibberellic acid or other growth-stimulating plant or chemical
- thermometer
- fluorescent lamp or plant lamps
- meterstick or tape measure
- graph paper
- electronic balance or postal scale (optional)

Procedure

1. Germinate 45 to 50 pea seeds by putting them inside moist paper towels or sawdust. Keep them warm and dark, with a bowl inverted over them to keep in the moisture. Only the seeds that germinate will be used in this experiment.

> Do not select ungerminated seeds. You are studying the effect of the stimulant on growing plants, not on germinating seeds—although you could design an experiment to do that, too.

2. While the seeds are germinating, start your notebook. You will record every

detail of your experiment, including (a) the date you bought the gibberellic acid or other growth stimulant (in case the compound should deteriorate with time), (b) the date on which the peas were placed in the towels for germination, (c) the temperature, (d) the date of planting, (e) when the acid was first administered, (f) the date of the second treatment, and so on.

3. When the peas have germinated, fill 32 paper drinking cups to within 1 cm of the rim with sifted topsoil or potting soil moistened just enough to form a crumbly lump when a pinch of it is squeezed.

4. Place one sprouted pea in each cup so that the tip of the shoot is pointing up and flush with the surface of the soil.

5. Arrange the cups in eight groups of four and label according to the concentration of gibberellic acid the group is to receive: 5%, 0.5%, 0.05%, 0.005%, 0.0005%, 0.00005%, and 0.000005%. One group of four cups is reserved as a control and receives only tap water. Label these cups "control."

Labeled cups

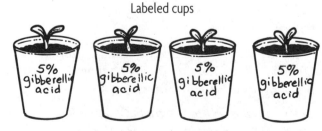

Hydroponic tank with different media

6. In one of the dropper bottles, dissolve 2.5 g of the gibberellic acid in 50 cc or 50 mL of tap water. Label this

bottle "full strength (5%)." This is approximately a 5 percent solution by weight. The gibberellic acid will not be sold in pure form, but will be mixed with some inert substance.

7. In a second dropper bottle, prepare the second dilution by putting 5 cc of the 5 percent solution in the bottle and adding enough tap water to make 50 cc. Label this bottle "0.5%." Each cubic centimeter of this solution contains one-tenth as much gibberellic acid as the 5 percent solution.

8. Place 5 cc of the 0.5 percent solution in a third bottle and add water to make 50 cc. Label this bottle "0.05%."

9. Continue this process until seven dilutions have been prepared. Label each bottle to indicate the dilution it holds: 0.05%, 0.005%, and so on (see step 5). Fresh dilutions must be prepared for each treatment, because the acid gradually loses its activity in solution.

Inert chemicals in products have no effect. They are there as filler or are left over from the production process.

The old name for commercial gibberellic acid is Brellin. If you use Brellin no. 10, each milliliter contains 5 mg of gibberellic acid; hence each cubic centimeter or milliliter of the 5 percent solution will contain a 0.25 mg of acid.

Seven dilutions

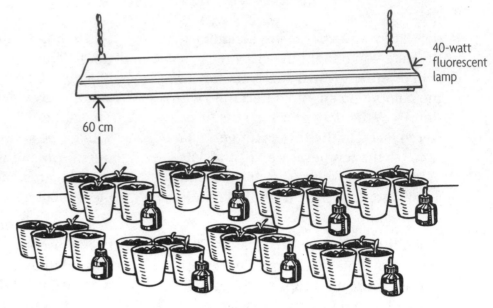

40-watt fluorescent lamp

60 cm

10. To eliminate the influence of variations in environment during the experiment, place the growing plants in a dark room in which the temperature does not vary appreciably from 20° C. The plants should be exposed daily for 11 hours to a fluorescent lamp or plant lamp of at least 40 watts placed lengthwise above the cups at a height of 60 cm. Each experimental plant should receive a treatment with 10 cc of the appropriate fresh acid dilution, as indicated by its label, every 48 hours for at least 14 days. No water or other solution should be administered—except to the four control plants, which receive 10 cc of tap water. The acid should always be administered in a uniform manner. Pour the dilutions on the soil near the base of the plant.

11. Record the height of each plant daily, beginning with 0 cm on the day the experiment starts, when the shoots are flush with the top of the soil. Make a table in your notebook with columns for recording the date and the height of each plant.

12. Plot graphs of the plant growth, either for each individual plant or for averages of each group. Construct similar tables for the number of leaves or other measurable quantities you identify.

At the end of the experiment, you can measure the final weights of the plants with an electronic balance.

13. As an extension, you can explore the effect of gibberellic acid on the growth of other plant types, such as algae, molds, mushrooms, mosses, or ferns. See chapter 8, "Growing Algae.")

References

Down to Earth: Garden Secrets! Garden Stories! Garden Projects You Can Do! by Michael J. Rosen (Orlando, Fla.: Harcourt Brace, 1998).

Green Thumbs: A Kid's Activity Guide to Indoor and Outdoor Gardening by Laurie Carlson (Chicago: Chicago Review Press, 1995).

Let's Grow It: Funstation by Brenda Walpole (San Diego: Advantage/Silver Dolphin, 1998).

Sensitive Plants

Plants respond to different stimuli, including light, gravity, water, nutrients, and touch. Flowers grow toward the Sun. Roots push downward into the soil. Peas and beans have tendrils that wrap around a trellis and help them climb. Usually, plants move slowly, by growing. A plant bends or twines over a period of hours or days because one side grows faster than the other—the outer, faster-growing side curls around the inner, slower-growing side.

Some plants move much faster, however. Their movement is not due to growth, but to an immediate chemical response, much the way an animal's muscle moves in response to touch. The most famous sensitive plant is the Venus's-flytrap. This plant is a **carnivore** (meat eater), trapping tiny flies in its clawlike trap and digesting them. There are many other species of sensitive plants that move in response to touch, in order to trap insects or as a defensive response. Most sensitive plants are semitropical or tropical.

> The Venus's-flytrap gets nutrients from flies rather than from the soil.

Venus's-flytrap
(*Dionaea muscipula*)

catclaw mimosa
(*Mimosa pigra*)

Sensitive plants

- toothpicks
- notebook and pencil
- straw
- tissue paper
- white paper
- protractor
- graph paper
- cuticle scissors
- eyedropper
- assorted liquids (water, oil, rubbing alcohol, nail polish remover, etc.)
- Q-tips

> Some carnivorous plants, such as the sundew (*Drosera aliciae*) and pitcher plant (*Cephalotus follicularis*), trap insects with sticky goo and slippery sloping surfaces. You can feed them insects or small bits of hamburger with a pair of tweezers.

Materials

- 1 or more sensitive plants, such as catclaw mimosa (*Mimosa pigra*), sensitive plant (*M. pudica*), Venus's-flytrap (*Dionaea muscipula*), wild sensitive pea (*Cassia nictitans*), or bladderwort (*Utricularia purpurascens* or U. *roseopurpurea*) (available from a nursery or catalog)

Procedure

1. Identify the part of the plant that is sensitive to touch, triggering a response. You can use a toothpick to gently touch different parts of the plant to see what part responds. In the case of the Venus's-flytrap, small hairs inside the trap will cause it to close when stimulated. In the wild sensitive pea, look for a pulvinus, an enlargement at the base of the leaflet and at the base of the leaf stem. Determine how long it takes your plant to return to its normal, untriggered state.

The pulvinus is a special motor organ. The center of the pulvinus contains a strand of vascular (vein-containing) tissue. Fluid pressure inside the plant helps it to sense its surroundings and move.

2. You can conduct various experiments to test the sensitivity of your plant. Keep a detailed log of all your activities and experiments.

   a. Determine the degree of physical stimulation needed to trigger a response: Use a small straw to drop different size balls of tissue paper onto the triggering mechanism. What is the minimum **mass** (measure of matter) required to achieve a triggering response? Do larger forces cause the leaves or trap to move through greater angles? Use paper, pencil, and a protractor to make a **goniometer** like the one shown, to measure the angle of closing traps or curling leaves. Graph your results, showing the angle as a function of the mass.

   b. Determine whether the level of water or light affects the response: Repeat the experiment in step 2a, but use a constant mass and change the amounts of light and water present. (Be sure to test these variables one at a time, not simultaneously, so that you know which created the effect. Let an hour pass after making your light or water

changes, to allow the plant to adjust to the new environment.) Does the plant respond differently at night? When wet or dry? Again, you can measure the extent of movement with a goniometer.

   c. Determine the effect of certain organs on the response: Cut the trigger hairs or pulvinus from your plant with cuticle scissors and see how it responds without these organs.

   d. Determine whether the plant responds to chemical stimuli: You can use an eyedropper to administer common household liquids, such as water, alcohol, oil, and so on. You can examine the effect of vapors by using a Q-tips swab dipped in a liquid and held close to, but not touching, your plant. Rubbing alcohol (isopropyl alcohol) and nail polish remover (acetone in water) have vapors that **evaporate** (change from a liquid to a vapor) readily into the air. *Avoid inhaling the vapors of these liquids.*

References

Carnivorous Plants (Lerner Natural Science series) by Cynthia Overbeck and Kiyoshi Shimizu (Minneapolis: Lerner, 1989).

Meat-Eating Plants (Weird and Wacky Science series) by Nathan Aaseng (Berkeley Heights, N.J.: Enslow, 1996).

Sundew Stranglers: Plants That Eat Insects by Jerome Wexler (New York: Dutton, 1995).

Carnivorous plant database: www.hpl.hp.com/bot/cp_home

11.25° each
1 2 3 4 5 6 7 8 9 10 11 12 13 14 15 16

reference line

Goniometer

8 Growing Algae

How would you like to be a chemist, optician, taxonomist, histologist, geneticist, and hydroponicist all at once? You can if you grow **algae.** The science of growing these fascinating aquatic, plantlike organisms overlaps with many fields. Algae range in size from microscopic single cells to kelps (seaweed) nearly as tall as an oak tree. Some algal species can live in boiling natural springs; others thrive in the polar wastes; still others are found at great ocean depths at the heated openings of **geothermal** (heat energy supplied by Earth) vents.

Chemistry is the study of the nature of matter. **Optics** is the study of light. **Taxonomy** is the systematic classification of organisms. **Histology** is the study of tissue structure in organisms. **Genetics** is the study of inheritance of **traits** (features of an organism, such as hair color). **Hydroponics** is the method of growing life forms in nutrient broths. (see chapter 5, "Hydroponics").

Materials

- metric measuring spoons and cup
- plant fertilizer (e.g., Miracle-Gro)
- saucepan
- stove or hot plate (*requires adult help*)
- narrow glass jar
- dropper bottles
- butter knife
- film canisters or other small containers
- notebook and pencil
- Petri dishes or jar lids
- microscope or magnifying glass
- paper

Procedure

1. Start the preparation of your nutrient broth by mixing 5 mL of plant fertilizer with 500 mL of tap water in a saucepan.

2. Ask an adult to boil your broth on high heat for about 10 minutes or until it boils down to 250 mL, whichever happens first. Allow the broth to cool for 10 minutes.

3. Transfer the liquid carefully to a 1-L glass jar that has been washed in warm, soapy water, rinsed, and dried.

4. Collect algae-rich water from a local source. Be sure your collection equipment and containers are sterilized by washing them in soapy water and thoroughly drying them or running them through the dishwasher. That way you will be less likely to contaminate your

---

Algal blooms have occurred in many bodies of water due to fertilizer runoff from farms and lawns. The excessive growth of algae leads to **eutrophication,** a reduction of the oxygen supply. This is followed by the death of fish and other water-dwelling creatures, causing severe harm to the aquatic ecology.

Collecting algae

samples. The best place to find algae is in a small cove in a pond with green, scummy, stagnant water. Slow-moving streams work, too. You can collect water samples from the surface using a dropper bottle for each sample You can scrape green algae from a rock using a butter knife and transfer the sample to a film canister or other small container. You can also collect algae directly from the soil, scooping a sample into a film canister. Keep your samples wet or moist in their containers, at an even temperature. The faster you transport them, the better. Make sure to keep notes on where each sample originated.

5. Add a small specimen of each sample to a Petri dish filled with the nutrient broth you made in steps 1 to 3. (If you can't get Petri dishes, use jar lids that have been through the dishwater on a hot cycle. Use them right after they come out and have cooled down.)

6. Allow your specimens to **bloom** (become densely populated with microorganisms) over several days. Try to store the specimens in a location with temperature and light conditions similar to those where you collected the original samples.

7. Using a microscope or a magnifying glass, you may be able to sort the algae

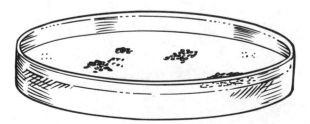

Algal bloom in a Petri dish

Each year, we can grow 14.7 tons of algae per hectare used for algae cultivation. Why would anyone want to grow algae? This industry has many potential uses, from producing materials for the pharmaceutical industry to designing oil-eating algae to help clean up tanker spills.

by type with a clean dropper. Try to find one or a few growths that are identical, and carefully transfer them to a new, clean nutrient-broth dish. Allow this algae sample to bloom. This should be a "pure" sample of one alga type.

8. You can transfer algae to a sheet of paper and let them dry. Then mark the paper with the date, time, and place you found the sample.

The leaflike parts of many algae consist of only two layers of cells coated with a clear substance. When the algae dry on paper, they seem to have no thickness and look like lines drawn with ink in exotic colors.

9. You can perform experiments on algae to see how well different types grow under different conditions, varying the fertilizer type, light source, or temperature.

References

Pond Water Zoo: An Introduction to Microscopic Life by Peter Loewer and Jean Jenkins (New York: Athenuem, 1996).

Ponds and Pond Life (Nature Detective series) by Anita Ganeri (Danbury, Conn.: Franklin Watts, 1993).

Microbe Zoo:
www.commtechlab.msu.edu/sites/dlc-me/zoo/

The Pleasures of Pond Scum:
www.sciam.com/1998/0398issue/0398amsci.html

Cultivating Slime Molds

Slime molds are primitive organisms that do not fit neatly into the categories of animal, vegetable, or mineral. They resemble both **amoebae** (single-cell organisms) and fungi. Like amoebae, slime molds are bloblike and move around to find food or avoid danger. Like a fungi, they release spores that feed on microorganisms and decaying organic matter. As the slime mold moves, it consumes food, produces waste, and grows. Slime molds like cool, moist conditions—you'll find them on the forest floor or on blades of grass, especially in locations where it is damp, such as near a streambed under a thick canopy of trees. Slime molds have a preference for upright objects, such as grass, tree stumps, and walls. Once you learn to recognize slime molds, you can collect and cultivate them.

There are over 450 known species of amoeboid slime molds. *Myxomycophya* is a common genus of slime mold. Some biologists argue that slime molds are neither plant nor animal, because they are unique in their structure and behavior.

Materials

- Petri dish (or inverted saucer or peanut butter jar lid)
- 2 Pyrex pie plates or a clear lidded casserole
- filter paper or paper towel (coffee filter paper)
- distilled water
- rubber tubing
- utility scissors
- metric ruler
- slime mold samples (You may be able to collect slime mold samples from a wooded area. You can also obtain slime mold cultures from a science equipment supplier—see page 1. Transport your samples in a clean, dry jar, as quickly as possible.)
- oats (Use old-fashioned rolled oats, not the "quick" variety.)
- notebook and pencil
- colored pencils
- assorted cereals or fruit
- assorted liquids (vinegar, rubbing alcohol, nail polish remover)
- eyedropper

Two suggested choices are *Physarium polycephalum* or *Myxomycophyta.*

Procedure

To Cultivate Your Slime Mold

1. Place a Petri dish within a larger, clear, covered container, such as a casserole or a pair of facing Pyrex pie plates.

2. Lay a sheet of filter paper or a paper towel across the Petri dish. The paper should droop to the bottom of the dish.

3. Wet the paper thoroughly with distilled water, pouring off the excess. From time to time during the experiment, add enough water to prevent drying.

filter paper

Petri dish

2 Pyrex pie plates

4 spacers cut from rubber tubing

Chamber for cultivating slime mold

> Distilled water should be used to prevent contamination by other microorganisms or harmful minerals.

4. Make spacers from rubber tubing, using utility scissors to cut three or four 2.5-cm lengths of tubing. Pass the scissors through each piece of tubing, making one straight cut along the length so that you can pull the tubing open and fasten it to the rim of the pie plate as shown. Space the pieces evenly around the circumference to allow for a small air gap.

5. Place a small fragment of slime mold on the paper and wet it with a drop of water. Within a few hours the organism will awaken from its deathlike state. Keep the unused organisms in the refrigerator.

6. When the slime mold has emerged and has begun to seek food, put a flake of moistened uncooked oats in contact with the rapidly spreading growth.

7. Keep the covered dish at room temperature in an area that does not get direct sunlight. As the slime mold increases in size, place more oat flakes along the growth front. A rapidly moving specimen will consume a larger number of oat flakes than a sluggish one. In either case, the feeding organism will show a decided preference for fresh oat flakes and will abandon partially digested ones. Flakes that have first been moistened with a drop of water are accepted more readily than dry oats. To maintain a clean culture, transfer the organisms to a fresh sheet of filter paper or paper towel weekly, avoid overfeeding, and remove abandoned food that shows signs of becoming moldy or slimy.

*To Perform Experiments
on Your Slime Mold*

1. What is the life cycle of your slime mold? Research this in depth and sketch what you believe corresponds to the different life stages in your slime mold. Keep a log with colored pencils.

In the early stage of growth, the myxomycete is like an animal, and generally consists of an unattractive patch of naked **protoplasm** (the contents of the nucleus of a living cell). Over time it develops colorful **sporangia,** or fruiting bodies, that release spores into the air. This is how this type of slime mold reproduces. The stage can be induced at any time by removing most of the food and allowing the myxomycete to roam while simultaneously keeping the organism moist. The transformation will occur suddenly, usually at night, within a week or two. If the observer is fortunate enough to witness the actual transformation, he or she will see the entire myxomycete, now more orange than yellow, appear to separate into uniformly rounded masses that ascend from the surface on stalks and then develop into weird, multilobed bodies.

2. Explore food preferences. What does your slime mold like to eat? Try different types of cereal or fruit (e.g., strawberries). Measure its rate of migration and compare its preferences for different foods.

3. Experiment with toxins and irritants: How does the slime mold respond to vinegar (acetic acid), rubbing alcohol (isopropyl alcohol), and nail polish remover (acetone)? Place a drop of each liquid next to the slime mold in three trials and study the slime mold's behavior.

References

Myxo web site:
www.wvonline.com/myxo/

Introduction to the Slime Molds:
www.ucmp.berkeley.edu/protista/
slimemolds.html

10 Learning Behavior in Sow Bugs

Sow bugs make interesting scientific subjects. This common creature, *Porcellio laevia*, lives in moist places almost everywhere. The adult is about 1 cm long. The body consists of seven free segments, each of which bears a pair of legs. Sow bugs, like other organisms, must develop learned behavior to survive. Important types of learned behavior include finding food and water, finding shelter, and avoiding dangerous conditions of temperature or toxins—to name a few.

Sow bugs must conserve bodily water or they dry out and die. Because of this, they avoid light. You can teach sow bugs to run through a maze to avoid light.

Sow bug

Materials
- 450-g coffee can with plastic lid
- sand
- leaf mold
- potatoes
- water
- sponge
- pushpin
- sow bugs
- notebook and pencil
- a test tube for each sow bug
- peat moss
- paper towels
- cotton balls
- pen and masking tape (for labeling test tubes)
- metric ruler
- scissors
- cardboard
- household epoxy or cement
- clear plastic storage box with lid about 8 cm wide by 11 cm long by 1.5 cm deep
- utility knife (*requires adult help*)
- 2 wood blocks, each 5 by 1 by 1 cm
- 100-watt light
- timer

Procedure

To Prepare the Setup

1. Before collecting sow bugs, you should construct a culture chamber. Fill a 450-g coffee can halfway with a mixture consisting of one part sand by volume to two parts leaf mold. On this surface, place a peeled raw potato and a damp

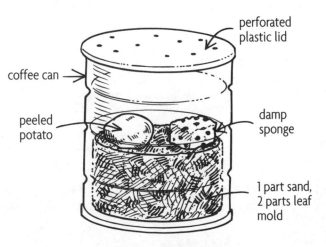

Sow bug culture chamber

sponge of about the same size. (Replace the potato and moisten the sponge every 2 or 3 days.) Close the container with a perforated cover which you can make by using a push-pin to punch numerous holes in the plastic lid.

2. Find some sow bugs. They can be found under rocks and logs. The insects may be scarce in winter and when the weather is hot and dry. In cities, they tend to hide together in the damp cellars of apartment buildings under wooden boxes or old newspapers. How do you identify sow bugs? It's easy, once you understand how they got their nickname "pill bugs." Touch one, and it curls up into a little ball to protect itself.

> If your search for sow bugs is unsuccessful, try making a trap by hollowing out a potato and placing it under a tree or shrub. Cover the potato with a few leaves and come back after 48 hours. The trap will usually contain several lively specimens. But don't use this strategy indoors—you may attract some less desirable creatures.

3. Put your sow bugs in the culture chamber.

4. Have your notebook ready for recording training results. During training, specimens must be kept in individual containers. These containers can consist of test tubes filled halfway with peat moss or leaf

mold and covered with a piece of paper towel. Place a sliver of fresh potato on the towel along with the bug. Plug the containers loosely with tufts of damp cotton balls and label them with numbers or names so that each bug can be distinguished from the others. Replace the potato as necessary and keep the cotton moist.

5. Construct the apparatus in which the bugs are trained. Measure and cut cardboard partitions and cement them in place in a clear plastic box so that they form a T shape of passages that are 1 cm wide. Have an adult use a utility knife to cut 1-cm-square openings in the walls of the box at the base of the T and at each end of the crossarm. Two blocks of wood that make a loose fit with the openings must be provided for closing either or both openings of the crossarm.

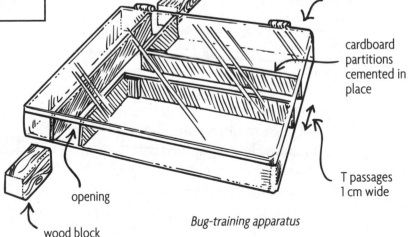

clear plastic box with lid

cardboard partitions cemented in place

T passages 1 cm wide

opening

wood block

Bug-training apparatus

Run the Experiment

1. First determine and record the natural turning preference of each bug. Most sow bugs will take a preferred path through the passageway. Having crawled up the leg of the T, some will habitually turn into the right portion of the crossarm and others into the left. Some will show no preference. During the second phase of the experiment, the bugs are trained to turn in the direction contrary to their natural preference.

2. Begin the experiment by transferring five or six specimens from the culture chamber to labeled individual containers Then remove a bug from a selected container, and, holding it lightly between your thumb and forefinger, let it crawl from your fingertip into the opening at the base of the T. Record the direction of the turn, right or left. A sow bug can tolerate only about 10 runs a day without suffering ill effects. For this reason, the 20 runs needed to establish a reliable estimate of turning preference should span 2 days.

3. Training is accomplished by running each specimen through the course and punishing "wrong" behavior. Each time a bug makes a turn in the direction it naturally prefers, immediately plug all exits with wood blocks and hold a 100-watt incandescent light close to the top of the passageway for about 20 seconds. When the bug runs in the direction opposite to its natural preference, plug the exit of the runway for 20 seconds, but do not expose the animal to the punishing light. Use your notebook to keep details of each training run: (a) the bug involved, (b) the exact conditions, (c) the results, and (d) your conclusions about sow bug learning.

4. The training runs must be spaced at least 5 minutes apart. Between runs, return the subjects to their individual containers to "think it over." The training

> Statistically it can be shown that nine consecutive correct turns will occur by chance only once in 100 runs.

period should normally take 3 to 10 days, depending on how quickly the individual learns. Remember, do not subject the bug to more than 10 training runs a day. At the conclusion of the training phase, nine consecutive correct turns are evidence that the bug has learned. A correct turn is defined as one made in the direction opposite to the bug's natural preference as determined by the first phase of the experiment.

5. Take your best learners and see whether you can train them to fetch a stick, roll over, or walk a tightrope. Then you can start your own sow bug circus! (Just kidding.)

References

Bugs (book and CD-Rom) by Gerald Legg and Philippa Moyle (Smithmark Publishing and Factfinders Interactive Multimedia, 1998).

Pet Bugs: A Kid's Guide to Catching and Keeping Touchable Insects by Sally Kneidel (New York: John Wiley & Sons, 1994).

Slugs, Bugs, and Salamanders: Discovering Animals in Your Garden by Sally Kneidel (Golden, Colo.: Fulcrum, 1997).

11 Breeding Butterflies

Butterflies and moths are insects in the order Lepidoptera. They have six legs, four wings, two antennae, a head, thorax, and abdomen. Nothing brings beauty to a warm day like a swallowtail fluttering over a flower, or a group of monarchs migrating overhead.

> There are thousands of species of butterflies, and hundreds of thousands of species of moths. Butterflies fly by day and have clubbed antennae; moths fly at night and do not have clubbed antennae.

There are four stages in the life cycle of butterflies and moths—egg, **larva, pupa,** and adult. The most dramatic stage of the life cycle is the moment when the adult emerges from its cocoon (the pupa's protective silk covering). The butterfly's cocoon is called a **chrysalis.** You can breed moths and butterflies with some care. With luck you may even witness an adult female in the act of laying her eggs.

Materials

- craft sticks
- wire or plastic screen
- meterstick
- utility scissors
- needle and thread (Bottom thread works best.)
- glue
- caterpillar
- notebook and pencil
- field guides to insects and plants
- tight-fitting gloves
- small paper bag

Caterpillar feeding

- string
- pruning shears

> A certain species of the giant silkworm moth from India, *Antheraea mylitta,* is one of the world's largest insects, weighing about 45 g as an adult. The adult moth is bigger than your hand! An egg the size of a match head can develop into a 25-cm moth. Specimens caught in the Philippine Islands have a wingspan of 30 cm—as long as your forearm.

Procedure

1. In preparation for butterfly and moth breeding, construct a small cage from craft sticks and screen. You can use wire or plastic screen. The dimensions of the cage are 20 by 20 by 40 cm. Cut the screen with utility scissors and use needle and thread to attach it to a craft stick frame. The craft sticks can be connected to one another with glue, or simply sewn to the screen for support as shown on next page.

2. Look for caterpillars in a park, meadow, or on your own property if it has trees and shrubs. Check leaves, both the tops and undersides. In particular, keep your eyes open for leaves that have bite marks indicating creatures have been munching there.

3. When you find a caterpillar, take notes on it: color, size, markings, and other distinctive information. Look your insect up in a field guide. Also, make note of the plant where it was found. You'll need to go back and take more fresh twigs from the plant later on. If

> Be careful when handling caterpillars. You should handle them gently. Gypsy moth caterpillars have little bristles that can cause a minor skin rash. However, you are more of a threat to the caterpillar than it is to you. Protect both yourself and your small friend by wearing tight-fitting gloves.

you're not sure what kind of plant it is, take a sample of the leaves and stems to identify the plant later, using a field guide.

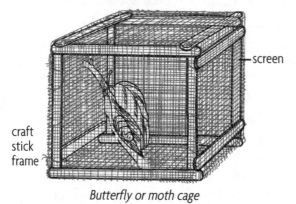

craft stick frame

screen

Butterfly or moth cage

4. Put a paper bag over the twig or weed on which your specimen is feeding and tie the end closed with string so that the insect cannot escape. Cut the twig off the plant with pruning shears and bring it home.

5. Look inside the bag a day or so later. You may discover that all the leaves have been eaten. If so, shift the caterpillar to a fresh batch of the same kind of leaves and tie the paper bag over it. You may have to repeat this transfer several times.

6. Eventually you will find that your specimen has vanished and a cocoon has begun to take its place. Make note of the caterpillar's methods in building the cocoon and how long it spends in the process. When the cocoon is complete, break off the twig to which it is attached and transfer it to the small cage.

7. Place the cage outdoors in a location matching as closely as possible the site where you found the insect. After days or weeks—depending upon the species and the season of the year—the adult will emerge from the cocoon, and you will have the thrill of discovering the exotic creature your caterpillar was destined to become.

> Some species prefer sunny locations; others do best in shade.

8. Release your young pet almost immediately into the wild. Its wings could become permanently damaged if it bangs them against the walls of the small cage. The best place to release your butterfly or moth is where you originally found the caterpillar. Release it in pleasant weather, perhaps on a cool, sunny morning, with no wind, to introduce your winged friend to the world on a gentle note.

References

Butterfly and Moth (Eyewitness Books) by Paul Whalley (New York: Random Library, 1989).

The Butterfly Book: A Kid's Guide to Attracting, Raising, and Keeping Butterflies by Kersten Hamilton (Santa Fe, N.M.: John Muir, 1997).

Butterflies of North America: www.npwrc.usgs.gov/resource/distr/lepid/bflyusa/bflyusa.htm

Children's butterfly site: www.mesc.usgs.gov/butterfly/butterfly.html

Monarch Watch: www.MonarchWatch.org/

Unraveling the Secrets of Marchs: www.sciam.com/0997issue/0997amsci.html

Hummingbird Studies

Biology 12

Hummingbirds are the smallest of birds. The calliope hummingbird weighs about 2.5 g—the weight of a dime. You could mail a dozen of them by first-class mail for 33 cents (although it would not be very nice). Hummingbirds, like bees and butterflies, live on the nectar of flowering plants. With simple preparations you can

> **Nectar** is a sweet liquid produced by flowers to attract pollinating insects and animals.

attract, feed, and study hummingbirds in your own backyard. Although commercial hummingbird feeders and food are widely available, you can save money by using cheaper basic materials.

> The summer is the best time to study hummingbirds in the northern United States. The rufous hummingbird migrates all the way from Mexico to Alaska.

Materials

- plastic bottle with cap
- metric ruler
- piece of heavy plastic and a rubber band (if bottle cap is unavailable)
- drill with 3-mm drill bit (*requires adult help*)
- small file
- paintbrush and red or yellow paint
- red food coloring (if not using paint)
- sugar
- water
- metric scale
- string
- duct tape
- hanging postal scale or spring scale
- notebook and pencil
- graph paper
- juice samples
- camera with tripod and telephoto lens (optional)
- high-speed photographic film (optional)

Procedure

1. Construct a hummingbird feeder. A small plastic bottle will do. The taller and narrower, the better. The best dimensions are similar to those of a large test tube, perhaps 15 by 3 cm. Either use the cap that came with the bottle or construct a new one out of heavy plastic fastened with a rubber band over the mouth of the bottle. The cap will need to be removable. Ask an adult to drill one or two 3-mm holes in the cap that the hummingbird can fit its beak through to feed. (Don't make the holes too big, unless you want to build a bee and wasp feeder!) File the edges of the holes to ensure that they are not sharp.

> The best color for a feeder to attract hummingbirds is red. (Yellow is second best, but yellow may also attract unwanted insects.) You can either paint your feeder red or add red food coloring to the sugar-water mixture.

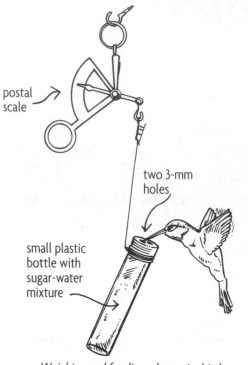

postal scale

two 3-mm holes

small plastic bottle with sugar-water mixture

Weighing and feeding a hummingbird

> The hummingbird has the highest metabolic rate of any warm-blooded animal. It can consume 30 times the daily rate of food intake by weight needed by a person doing physical labor.

2. Find out how much hummingbirds eat: Prepare your hummingbird food by mixing equal parts of sugar and water by weight, using a metric scale. (Use less sugar and more water if you want to attract fewer insects.) Fill the feeder and use the string and tape to hang it from a postal scale. (A light spring scale can be used, but is less desirable because it can be bouncy.) Study the feeder to see when the hummingbirds like to visit. Record the weight of the feeder, string, and tape before and after a hummingbird visits. The difference in weight tells you how much the little creature consumed. Record the feedings in a table indicating the time and weight consumed over several days. Graph your results.

> Don't use honey—it can breed a fungus harmful to the hummingbirds.

3. Find out what hummingbirds like to eat: Experiment with different solutions of juice, sugar, and water. Determine the optimal food based upon how often the hummingbirds visit, and how much solution they consume. Clean and refill your feeder frequently.

4. If you want, you can photograph hummingbirds. In order to get the best results, use a 35-mm camera with a telephoto lens and a tripod. Aim the camera at your feeder. Use high-speed film, such as ASA 400 or higher. If your camera has an automatic shutter speed, open the aperture as much as possible (the lower the f-stop, the wider the opening—1.4 is more open than 8). If your camera has an automatic aperture, reduce the shutter speed as much as possible. The lower the shutter speed, the less blurry your photos will be. A shutter speed of $\frac{1}{1,000}$ second will freeze motion much more effectively than $\frac{1}{30}$ second.

> Hummingbirds also eat small insects, and if you are skilled with your camera—and lucky—you might capture an image of one feasting this way.

References

A Dazzle of Hummingbirds by Bruce Berger, ed. Vicki Leon (Topeka, Kans.: Econo-Clad Books, 1999).

Hummingbirds (First Book series) by Mark J. Rauzon (Danbury, Conn.: Franklin Watts, 1997).

Hummingbird Society: www.hummingbird.org/

13 Raising Reptiles

Most people are afraid of snakes and other reptiles, and not without reason. After all, many reptiles are poisonous, and not everyone can immediately tell which are poisonous and which are not. But reptiles are interesting animals, and you can gain much pleasure from observing them.

Because reptiles have no internal mechanism to regulate their temperature, they must warm or cool themselves by means of their outside environment. They are said to be **ectotherms** (cold-blooded animals). Mammals and birds are **endotherms** (warm-blooded animals), meaning that they are able to maintain a body temperature in a very narrow range by an internal mechanism.

You can purchase many reptiles in pet stores. (We won't describe techniques for catching and handling them here, as that could be dangerous to both you and the reptile.) Ask the pet store personnel for their advice on care when you purchase your pet, and get a book or two on the subject. As some animal species are endangered, you should deal only with reputable stores.

It is not easy to study reptiles in nature. Most of them are shy animals that rapidly disappear at the approach of *Homo sapiens*.

Materials

- books about snakes or other reptiles
- 75-L aquarium or wooden box with glass front
- wire screen, perforated Masonite, Plexiglas with small air holes, or glass large enough to cover top of box
- Velcro tape
- plants
- metric ruler
- aquarium gravel
- scoop
- thermometer
- string
- duct tape
- incandescent lamp with fixture (A 75-watt reflective spotlight works well.)
- rocks, sticks, and other natural materials
- feeding materials (depending on species)
- baby liquid multivitamins

Procedure

1. Decide what reptile to get, and research it in advance. Make sure to choose a species that is safe, not too expensive, legal, and one that you will realistically be able to care for.

Good snake choices include bull, corn, fox, and rat snakes. Chameleons and turtles are other popular reptilian pets.

What is its habitat? What does it eat? What other creatures does it get along with? The species you choose determines all the rest of the steps of creating a dwelling and a diet plan.

2. Design your reptile's living structure. You can use an aquarium, or a wooden box with a glass front. With nonaquatic reptiles, it is necessary to cover the

box with a snug (but not airtight) cover. Snakes especially have a rare talent for finding a small opening. The cover can be a piece of wire screen, perforated Masonite, Plexiglas with small air holes, or glass slightly raised for ventilation. Secure the cover in place with Velcro tape.

Avoid using wire screen to cover a snake cage. Snakes have a tendency to rub their noses on the screen and injure themselves. For some of the stronger species of snake, a sturdy top is needed, perhaps with a weight or a clasp to hold it down.

3. Make your reptile feel at home. You want to be careful about adding too many things that will make the cage too wet or unsanitary, but with careful planning you can create an interesting environment for the enjoyment of both you and your cold-blooded friend. Depending on your reptile's needs, you can divide the cage climate into broad categories and create a set of zones

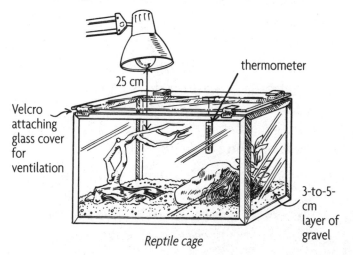

Velcro attaching glass cover for ventilation

25 cm

thermometer

3-to-5-cm layer of gravel

Reptile cage

appropriate to the species—for example, desert, temperate-zone region, or bog—and select plants and other surroundings that are compatible. You can research these environments in the library or on the Internet. Plants are a nice addition, but add them conservatively. For maximum sanitation, place a deep layer of washed aquarium gravel 3 to 5 cm in the bottom of the cage. From time to time, pick up excreta (waste) and contaminated gravel with

Some reptiles will burrow into the gravel.

a scoop. Properly managed, a reptile cage can be as decorative as the handsomest aquarium.

4. The illumination of the cage and the warmth it provides are important, both for the welfare of the animals and for satisfactory viewing. Most reptiles do best at temperatures slightly above 20°C, the desert species preferring temperatures as high as 38°C.

To monitor the temperature, hang a thermometer inside the cage from a string taped to the top edge of one wall. You can achieve good temperature control by balancing the heat of incandescent lamps against the heat loss through the sides of the cage and

You may notice a relationship between temperature and the level of reptilian activity. If your reptile is sluggish and rarely moves, raising the temperature may increase activity. But make sure to research the proper temperature range for your pet—you do not want to overheat a poor animal that is ordinarily slow in the wild.

by whatever air circulation there may be. Reptiles govern their body temperature by absorbing heat in varying amounts from their surroundings. An incandescent lamp at the top of the cage, such as a 75-watt reflective spotlight, together with the location of rocks or sticks at various distances from the light source, permit the animals to select their own temperature

It is astonishing to observe how quickly these not especially bright creatures learn that they can warm up most quickly by climbing to the highest point in the cage. When several lizards are in a cage and the light comes on after a cool night, an amusing scramble for top position usually ensues.

conditions. The incandescent spotlight will provide both **visible radiation** (light) and **infrared radiation** (heat). The radiation is concentrated toward the middle of the beam, however; it is therefore important to direct it so that the animal can get out of the beam and avoid overheating. Start by mounting the bulb so that the front of the bulb is about 25 cm from the highest piece of furniture in the cage.

5. Plan your reptile's diet. Few reptiles are vegetarians, although some turtle and lizard species will eat lettuce. The rest demand meat in various forms.

   a. Most turtles will eat any kind of meat offered, including a bit of your finger if you are not careful. Cod or ocean perch seem particularly tasty to aquatic turtles. Several of the more terrestrial (land-dwelling) species thrive on dog food. All

The turtle bowls sold with aquatic turtles are often inadequate. Such a turtle is properly kept in an aquarium measuring at least 25 by 30 cm. The aquarium should contain 15 to 20 cm of water, a sunning platform, and an ample heat source, such as the 75-watt spotlight mentioned in step 4. Be forewarned: these turtles will grow, some of them to the size of a dinner plate if they are properly nurtured.

aquatic turtles sold in pet stores are unable to eat when they are out of water.

   b. Most lizards are **insectivores,** eating moths, flies, beetles, grubs, grasshoppers, and so on. Such prey are not easy to come by in the

Mealworms, the larval form of the darkling beetle that commonly occurs around granaries, are a splendid food for insectivores, apparently supplying all the important trace nutrients.

winter, and it is almost impossible to convert a lizard to foods such as beef or fish. Mealworms and crickets can be bought in pet stores. It is not difficult to raise mealworms in amounts sufficient for one or two small lizards, but a larger lizard can put away 75 to 100 worms a week—make sure to budget for your pet's appetite! Crickets may be a better food choice for lizards. They are larger, more digestible, and more nutritious.

   c. Snakes are probably the most fascinating of all the reptiles. All snakes are carnivorous. In most cases, this means you must supply them with mice or rats for food (available at pet stores), although water and

> **Carnivores** eat meat.
> **Herbivores** eat plants.
> **Omnivores** eat both.
> Which are you?

ribbon snakes will eat fish (minnows or thawed pieces of frozen fish). Garter snakes can be induced to eat chopped earthworms mixed with hamburger; later they can be graduated to hamburger alone. Do not attempt to keep racers, coachwhips, or venomous snakes such as rattlers or copper-

> An unusually charming specimen is the red-bellied snake, which grows to a maximum length of 25 cm. It requires a steady diet of small angleworms or garden slugs (the brown ones, not gray), which are easily raised in leafy litter, with lettuce and chicken mash as food.

heads. The danger of getting bitten or poisoned is great.

d. Perhaps the most important item in the reptilian diet is an adequate vitamin supplement. Virtually all reptiles are sun worshipers, and in captivity they must have vitamin D to compensate for the lack of sunshine. Include one or two drops of

> Anoles and chameleons are very popular pets. With proper research, you can raise them with little difficulty. Chameleons have the fascinating ability to change their skin color to match their background, for purposes of camouflage.

baby liquid multivitamins per 30 mL of drinking water.

e. Water your reptiles properly. A snake will drink from any dish large enough to admit its head and an equal length of neck. Some lizards will drink from a dish; others, from a watering bottle. Some, such as the anoles, must be watered with a dropper or by sprinkling the plants in their habitat.

6. Introduce your reptile to its new home. Reptiles to be placed in a decorated cage should be carefully inspected for mites. Once introduced into such a cage, mites hide themselves in crevices and are almost impossible to eliminate.

7. Plan a scientific study of your reptile. You can do a behavior study to determine its optimal response to food, light, or terrain. Snakes shed their skin periodically. You can save your snake's skins to document its growth. Can you train your reptile to find food in a certain location or at a certain time of day?

References

Iguanas in Your Home: A Complete and Up-to-Date Guide (Basic Domestic Pet Library series) by R. M. Smith (New York: Chelsea House, 1997).

My Pet Lizards (All about Pets series) by Leeanne Engfer (Minneapolis: Lerner, 1999).

Snakes and Such (What a Pet series) by Alvin Silverstein, Virginia Silverstein, and Laura Silverstein Nunn (Chicago: Twenty-First Century Books, 1999).

Society for the Study of Amphibians and Reptiles:
www.ukans.edu/~ssar/ssar.html

Stereoscopic Vision

Have you ever wondered why humans and most other living creatures have two eyes instead of one? When you view things with both eyes, using **stereoscopic vision,** you have **depth perception.** This means that your brain takes information from both of your eyes and processes it into calculations of distance.

In certain instances, you can trick your brain into perceiving things in an unusual way—seeing depth when it is not really there, or inverting images. You can do this using a stereoscope or other optical devices, or by simply training your eyes with your fingers.

Materials

- paper, ruler, and pen or pencil
- stereoscope (available in science stores and museum gift shops)
- 4 small hand mirrors
- two 45-degree prisms
- cardboard boxes and mailing tubes
- sealing wax or Fun-Tak

Procedure

1. Sketch an illustration that suggests depth to the mind: Use your ruler to draw an 8-by-5-cm rectangle. Draw a horizontal line 1 cm from the top as shown. Now draw a series of disks that diminish in size from the lower left corner to the upper right. Make an effort to have the centers and radii line up as pictured. Common sense tells you that you have made a flat drawing. Yet your

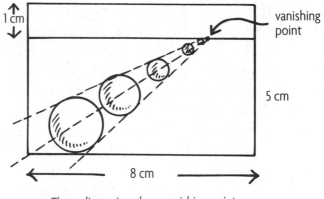

Three dimensions by a vanishing point

brain insists that it is a three-dimensional representation—especially if you shade the disks suggestively. Your brain gives you the impression of a series of spheres that run from the foreground to a vanishing point on the horizon.

> The painters of the Renaissance perfected this trick of representing three-dimensional reality in two dimensions.

2. Stereoscopic drawing is another method of representing three-dimensional reality in two dimensions, which creates an even more dramatic visual impression. Draw two rectangles, each

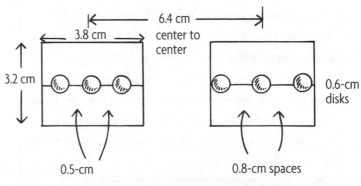

Three dimensions by stereoscopic drawing

3.8 by 3.2 cm. Space the rectangles about 6.4 cm apart from center to center. Now draw a horizontal line through the center of each, dividing the rectangles in half. Next make a shaded, 0.6-cm disk precisely in the center of each horizontal line. Flank the disk in the rectangle at left with an identical pair of disks spaced 0.5 cm from the circumference of the middle disk. Make a similar pair on the horizontal line of the rectangle at right, but space these disks 0.8 cm from the circumference. To the casual observer, there is certainly nothing in this drawing to suggest three dimensions. But when you view the drawing through a stereoscope, which causes the pair of rectangles to blend into a single image, the disk at left is seen as a sphere floating in space above the plane of the paper. The center disk will appear as a sphere in the plane of the paper, while the right one will seem to float in space behind the paper.

This is called wide-eyed stereoscopic seeing. You can also see the drawings in three dimensions without a stereoscope by the cross-eyed method. To achieve this you use only one finger. Place the drawing about 60 cm away, as before. Now put the tip of one index finger on the bridge of your nose, and while looking toward the drawing, slowly move your finger toward it, focusing your eyes on the tip. Again you will become conscious of four rectangles on the paper. Gradually, as your finger advances, the innermost pair of rectangles will fuse as in the wide-eyed method and you will see the center drawing in three dimensions. Note that the image is smaller and the two outermost spheres have inverted in their apparent orientation!

3. See if you can train your eyes to see the stereoscopic effect even without a stereoscope. View the drawing from about 60 cm away and place the index fingers of both hands just outside your eyes. Now, while continuing to look at the drawing, move your hands slowly toward the drawing. Your left eye will see the tip of your left index finger, and your right eye the tip of your right index finger. As your hands advance, you will become conscious of *four* rectangles on the paper. Your brain is accepting the independent images presented by each eye. The inner pair of images will gradually overlap. Finally they will blend. When this is accomplished, transfer your full attention to the fused image. It will appear in three dimensions, just as though it were seen through a stereoscope.

4. See if you can build these types of pseudoscopes.

Pseudo- means "false." A pseudoscope is a binocular-like device that enjoyed brief popularity shortly after Sir Charles Wheatstone (1802–75) invented the stereoscope in 1838. Pseudoscopes alter the way in which the eyes normally present information to the brain. Some exchange eye positions, so your right eye sees what the left one would, and vice versa. Others exaggerate the spacing between the eyes.

a. Hold up two hand mirrors, one somewhat to the left of the left eye, facing away from you at approximately a 45-degree angle, and the other in front of the right eye, parallel to the first mirror but facing you. The image reflected from the mirror at left should be directed into the

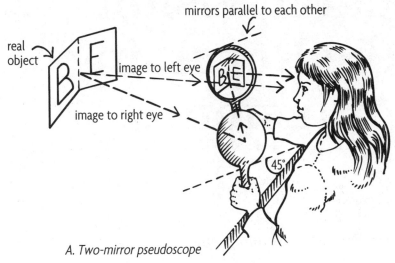

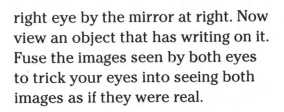

A. Two-mirror pseudoscope

boxes and mailing tubes, mounting the optic devices with sealing wax or Fun-Tak. For a real challenge, design your pseudoscope so it is adjustable for people with different eye widths.

right eye by the mirror at right. Now view an object that has writing on it. Fuse the images seen by both eyes to trick your eyes into seeing both images as if they were real.

b. View the same object through two right-angle prisms as shown. Notice the inversion of the writing—you are seeing an inverted world!

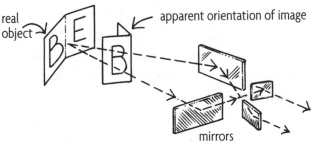

C. Four-mirror pseudoscope

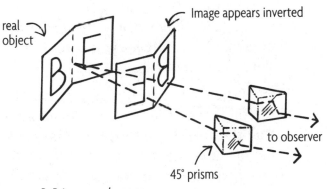

B. Prism pseudoscope

c. Set up a four-mirror pseudoscope as shown.

d. To make your pseudoscopes permanent and portable, mount the mirrors and prisms in some kind of holder. You can modify cardboard

References

How to Really Fool Yourself: Illusions for All Your Senses by Vicki Cobb (New York: John Wiley & Sons, 1999).

Now You See It, Now You Don't: The Amazing World of Optical Illusions, rev. ed., by Seymour Simon (Holt, Mich.: Beech Tree Books, 1998).

101 Amazing Optical Illusions: Fantastic Visual Tricks by Terry Jennings (New York: Sterling, 1998).

Optical Illusions (Scholastic Discovery Boxes series) by Kate Waters (New York: Scholastic Trade, 1996).

IllusionWorks:
www.illusionworks.com

Sandlot Science optical illusions:
www.sandlotscience.com/

15 Binocular Vision and the Reversing Cube Illusion

Biology

> **Binocular vision** is the ability to see with two eyes and determine depth.

Sometimes our senses fool us. This is the case with optical illusions: our eyes perceive things that are not there or that could not possibly exist. (See chapter 14, "Stereoscopic Vision," for more on optical illusions.)

Materials

- toothpicks or wire
- wood glue (if using toothpicks)
- cork or other small object

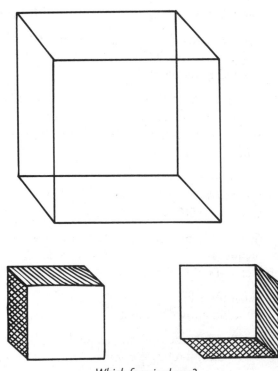

Which face is closer?

Procedure

1. Look at the cube pictured here. Nothing could be simpler. Which face of the cube is closest to you? At first one face appears closer—perhaps the lower—but if you stare at the cube for a moment, it will magically invert in your mind and then the opposite face will appear to be closer. Most people find the cube switches back and forth in perspective.

2. Construct a cube from 12 toothpicks and glue. First make two squares, then allow them to dry. Then stand them on end and glue on the remaining four edges. Add a toothpick as a handle protruding diagonally from one corner as shown. (Alternatively, you can make your cube from wire.)

3. Hold the handle vertically between the forefinger and thumb of one hand so that the cube is on top at normal reading distance. Close or cover up one eye. Look at the far corner of the cube. Within a matter of seconds the orientation of the cube will appear to reverse, as in the case of the perspective drawing. When the reversal occurs, pivot the handle slowly between the finger and thumb. The cube will appear to turn backward! Open the closed eye. The cube will instantly snap back to its true orientation.

Toothpick cube

With both eyes open, it is easier to judge depth because your brain analyzes the slightly different image received by each eye. Another clue to depth is the degree to which your eye must focus on objects. Other cues to depth include light and shade, and motion. Even with one eye you can judge distance to some degree.

4. Now hold the handle vertically with the cube on top as before. Again close one eye and fix attention on the far corner. When the illusion of reversal occurs, incline the cube away from you until the handle is horizontal. During this movement the handle will appear to bend at the point at which it is attached to the cube and the cube will swing upward until it seems to perch on one corner at the tip of the handle. When you pivot the handle, the cube will appear not only to turn in the wrong direction but also to rotate on its vertical axis as if driven by the handle through a pair of crown gears, which change the angle by 90 degrees.

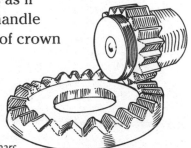

Crown gears

5. Equip the cube with a synchronous satellite. Place a small object such as a

A **synchronous satellite** is an object that orbits a body at a matching rate, such as one that remains at the same point above Earth's surface.

cork on a toothpick or wire and attach the toothpick or wire to the handle of the cube so that the cork is about 2.5 cm above the equator of the cube (assuming the south pole to be the corner to which the handle is attached). When the illusion of reversal occurs and the cube is rotated, the cube and its satellite will appear to move in opposite directions.

6. Turn the model rapidly and view it from different angles to discover other unexpected effects. Sometimes curves become evident when you do this.

7. Open both eyes, and the orientation of the cube remains clear—the inversion will stop.

Some people simply don't perceive the inversion described here. Everyone sees things in a slightly different way.

References

How to Really Fool Yourself: Illusions for All Your Senses by Vicki Cobb (New York: John Wiley & Sons, 1999).

Optical Illusion Magic: Visual Tricks and Amusements by Michael A. Dispezio (New York: Sterling, 1999).

IllusionWorks:
www.illusionworks.com

Sandlot Science optical illusions:
www.sandlotscience.com/

CHEMISTRY

16 Paper Chromatography

Analytical chemistry is a branch of science in which researchers separate mixtures into their fundamental parts: elements, compounds, and salts.

An **element** is a substance that contains atoms with the same number of protons. Elements are the purest substances you can produce chemically. A **compound** is formed by chemically joining atoms of two or more elements in definite whole-number ratios. A **salt** is a crystalline solid produced by the reaction of an acid with a base.

Chromatography (*chroma* means "color," and *graph* means "written") is an important technique in analytical chemistry for separating colored substances into individual pigments. You can easily perform chromatography with common household materials.

A **pigment** is a chemical that imparts color to materials. Most inks and fabrics have a blend of pigments that give them their appearance.

Materials

- scissors
- metric ruler
- safety goggles
- chromatography paper (Laboratory Whatman filter paper no. 1 is ideal for chromatography. Alternatively, you can use coffee filters, fine writing paper, or vertical strips of newsprint—blank newspaper.)
- clear drinking glass or beaker
- assorted pens and markers (Colored pen sets are good because they have several different colors of the same brand. Get both waterproof and water-soluble inks to study.)
- tap water
- stirring rod (wider than the mouth of the glass. Any thin rod will work, including a pen or pencil, a straightened large paper clip, or a butterfly clip.)
- paper clip
- eyedropper
- assorted liquid solvents (A good set of solvents would include distilled or filtered water, ammonia, rubbing alcohol, and nail polish remover.)
- timer
- saucepan
- stove or hot plate (*requires adult help*)

Ammonia is a dissolved gas. Rubbing alcohol contains isopropyl alcohol. Nail polish remover contains acetone. Alcohol and acetone are flammable and should be kept from spark, heat, and flames. *Do not inhale the vapors of these solvents.*

Procedure

To Make a Strip Chromatogram

1. Cut a 3-cm-wide strip of chromatography paper that is 2 cm longer than the height of the glass, approximately 12 cm long. Use a black, water-soluble pen or marker to draw a line across one end of the strip, 2 cm from the end.

2. Fill the glass with 1 to 2 cm of tap water.

3. Put on safety goggles. Carefully wrap the top of the chromatography paper

around a stirring rod and secure the paper in place with a paper clip.

4. Hold the rod next to the glass at the same height as the mouth of the glass. Adjust the strip of paper so that the height of the inked line is approximately 1 cm above the surface of the liquid.

5. Lower the strip into the glass and rest the rod across the mouth so that the end of the paper is in the water but the line is above it.

6. Allow the chromatogram to run. The liquid will soak upward into the paper, rising through the inked line. The liquid is drawn through the paper fibers by **capillary action,** the process by which liquids are drawn into narrow tubes. After a few minutes you will

Chromatography is the chemical process you are performing here. The image you produce on the paper in the process is a **chromatogram**.

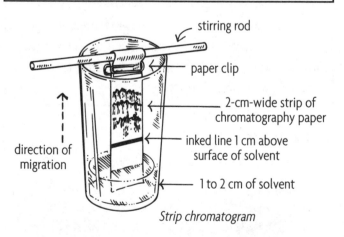

Strip chromatogram

- stirring rod
- paper clip
- 2-cm-wide strip of chromatography paper
- inked line 1 cm above surface of solvent
- 1 to 2 cm of solvent
- direction of migration

notice that the different pigments in the ink get carried upward at different rates. You will observe spacing of colors unique to that ink, like a fingerprint. When the migrating pigments approach the rod, remove the paper and allow it to dry on a flat, nonporous surface.

Pigments **migrate** (move into a surrounding **medium** or substance) at different speeds because of differences in their molecular properties: different **molecular weights** (the sum of the protons and neutrons in an atom), sizes, and chemical reactivity all contribute to their behavior. If you have a fluorescent light, you may be able to identify bands invisible to the human eye under ordinary conditions.

To Make a Circular Chromatogram

1. Lay a round piece of chromatography paper—10 cm in diameter—flat on a glass surface.

2. Make a 0.5-to-1.0-cm spot of ink in the center of the disk

"Solute" and "solvent" are terms that refer to solutions. The **solute** is the substance that dissolves; the **solvent** is the substance in which the solute dissolves. Together they form a **solution.** For instance, salt water is a solution of the solute called salt in the solvent called water. (For more on solvents and solutes, see chapter 18, "Growing Crystals.")

3. Put on safety goggles. Place a drop of solvent in the center of the ink spot. You can begin with distilled or filtered water, and repeat with other solvents in subsequent trials.

4. Add another drop of solvent every minute or so to make the chromatogram run toward the edges of the disk.

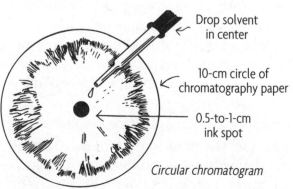

- Drop solvent in center
- 10-cm circle of chromatography paper
- 0.5-to-1-cm ink spot

Circular chromatogram

> This is a good method for analyzing substances already in liquid form, such as food coloring.

Experiments

1. Compare different colors of ink in a set of water-soluble pens of the same brand. Notice how dark colors such as black are really a mixture of many different pigments.

> When you mix red, blue, and green light together, you get white light (see chapter 32, "Color Addition"). But when you mix the corresponding colors of pigments together, you get black or brown. The first process is **color addition**—colored light rays are added to each other. The second process is **color subtraction**—colored light rays are **filtered** (blocked) out.

2. Isolate pigments by cutting apart your dry strip chromatogram (or several chromatograms run identically) into the component colors (cut between the color divisions). Redissolve the separate colored pigments in small quantities of water, in a saucepan. Have an adult boil off the water to get concentrated samples.

3. Vary the solvent, to see how the pigments separate under the influence of different liquids.

4. Vary the pens, to see how other types of ink perform. Some inks will not separate in some solvents.

5. Measure the rate of rise of the solvent, in millimeters per minute, and rates of individual pigments. The solvent normally rises between 1 and 10 mm per minute, depending on the temperature and the properties of the solvent.

> Other factors include the kind of paper used for the chromatogram, the orientation of the paper fibers, the length of the strip, the initial distance of the solvent from the starting line, the concentration of the mixture being analyzed, and the amount and kind of impurities present in both solvent and solute.

6. Stage a murder mystery in which you identify the murderer by his (or her) black pen. Use three or four black or blue pens of different brands, and produce the unique chromatograms associated with each brand. Although the inks may look the same when used for writing, they will certainly behave differently when you analyze them with chromatography.

> Bank checks that have been altered by the addition of words or numbers can often be detected by soaking off the suspected ink, separating its dyes, and comparing them with the dyes of the other ink on the check.

References

Janice VanCleave's A+ Projects in Chemistry: Winning Experiments for Science Fairs and Extra Credit, by Janice VanCleave (New York: John Wiley & Sons, 1993).

Janice VanCleave's Molecules (Spectacular Science Projects series) by Janice VanCleave (New York: John Wiley & Sons, 1993).

Science Projects about Kitchen Chemistry (Science Projects series) by Robert Gardner (Berkeley Heights, N.J.: Enslow, 1999).

The Lab of Shakashiri: www.scifun.chem.wisc.edu/scifun.html

17 Freezing and Thawing of Water and Salt

In winter salt is sprinkled on highways and sidewalks to melt sleet and snow, but in summer salt and water are mixed to freeze ice cream! The reason for this paradox is that salt lowers the melting point of water. There are several experiments you can conduct to demonstrate this effect.

Salt, or sodium chloride, is an **ionic solid** (a substance created when two or more elements react to form a fixed crystalline structure). The sodium and chlorine that make up sodium chloride are positive and negative ions. These charged particles grab water, which is **polar** (having a pair of charges that are equal and opposite). Because water has a positive and a negative side (hydrogen and oxygen), it is harder for the water molecules to bind to each other during freezing.

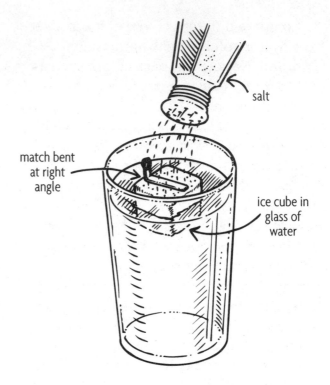

salt

match bent at right angle

ice cube in glass of water

Materials

- ice cubes
- glass
- water
- table salt
- book of matches
- mortar and pestle (optional)
- test tube or other small glass vial
- stirring rod
- thermometer (range at least –20° C to +120°C)
- notebook and pencil
- small bowl
- uninsulated copper wire

Procedure

1. Try this parlor trick: Float an ice cube in a glass of water. Have a shaker of salt within arm's reach. Hand a friend a paper match and challenge him or her to remove the ice cube from the water without lifting it with any implement other than the match. When your friend gives up, bend the head of the match at a right angle, place the body of the match flat on top of the ice, and cover the match with a thin layer of salt. The match will promptly freeze to the cube. Lift the cube from the glass by the head of the match.

> The salt melted some of the ice all around the edge of the match. Ions of sodium and chlorine gained freedom of motion when they dissolved in the film of water on the surface of the cube, and motion was induced by heat drawn from the ice. As a result, the temperature of the film of water in contact with the lower surface of the match dropped below the freezing point and turned into ice that cemented the cube to the match.

2. Crush some ice in a mortar and pestle (or by another method). Put it in a test tube or other small glass vial. Add a little water. Gently mix with a stirring rod. Take the temperature with the thermometer. It should be very close to 0°C, the melting point of pure water. Now add some salt and mix well. Record the new temperature. It should be lower. How low can you make the temperature go? Temperatures of –5°C or lower are possible in an amateur science lab. Quickly dip the bottom of the

> The lowest temperature Gabriel Fahrenheit (1686–1736) could obtain by mixing salt and ice was –17.8°C, or 0°F.

vial in some water in a bowl, then take it out. Frost will form on the outside as liquid water freezes to the colder surface.

3. Take a thin copper wire, about 15 to 20 cm long, from which the insulation, if any, has been removed. Place an ice cube on a table. Grasp each end of the wire so that your thumbs are about 5 cm apart. Push down on the ice cube with the wire. As you hold the wire, watch as it magically melts into the ice cube and the water freezes behind it. This refreezing after the removal of pressure is called **regelation.** You can actually pass the wire through the cube this way, leaving the cube intact.

> **Pressure** (force per unit area) also decreases the melting point of water.

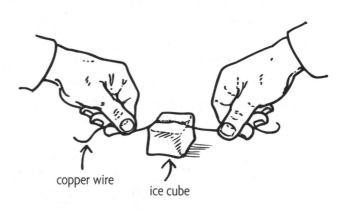

copper wire   ice cube

References

Adventures with Atoms and Molecules: Chemistry Experiments for Young People (Adventure with Science, Nos.1–5) by Robert C. Mebane and Thomas R. Rybolt (Berkeley Heights, N.J.: Enslow, 1998).

 Growing Crystals

Crystals are solids that form with a regular pattern of molecules connected together. A collection of atoms called the **unit cell** repeats over and over again, so that the crystal has a visible form similar to its atomic structure, the shape taken by its microscopic parts. The underlying structures of crystal forms are called **crystal systems.** There are six common crystal systems (see figure). Most **soluble** (able to dissolve in liquid) household solids, such as salt and sugar, will form crystals under the right conditions.

> **Minerals** are chemical elements and compounds that occur naturally as products of inorganic processes. Common mineral crystals include quartz, copper, diamond, amethyst, and garnet. Crystals of gold are sometimes found in quartz.

cubic

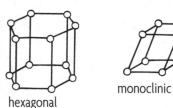

hexagonal

monoclinic

tetragonal

orthorhombic

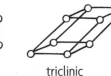

triclinic

Crystal systems and forms

Materials

- miscellaneous solids, including baking soda, sugar, and salt
- microscope or magnifying glass
- metric measuring cup
- distilled water (available at a supermarket)
- saucepan
- small spoon
- stove or hot plate (*requires adult help*)
- clear drinking glass
- small stainless steel washer or other weight
- 15-to-20-cm string
- stirring rod (or a pencil or chopstick)
- notebook and pencil
- postal or metric scale

Procedure

1. Begin with baking soda (sodium bicarbonate). Study this powder under the microscope or magnifying glass to see whether any crystal form is detectable.

2. Dissolve as much baking soda as you can in 200 mL of distilled water in a saucepan by adding the baking soda gradually with a small spoon and stirring.

3. Have an adult heat the solution gently until you can see vapor wisping off the top, but not to a full boil.

> The solute is the solid that you are dissolving. The solvent is the liquid in which it dissolves. Together they form a solution. The more solute you add, the more **concentrated** the solution becomes. When no more solute will dissolve, the solution is **saturated.**

4. Remove the solution from the heat and dissolve as much more baking soda as you can, again adding the powder slowly.

5. Allow the solution to cool, then pour it into a clear drinking glass.

6. Tie a small stainless steel washer to one end of a 15-to-20-cm string. Tie the other end of the string to the middle of a stirring rod. Rest the rod across the mouth of the glass and adjust the string so that it hangs down into the solution.

7. Put the glass in a place where it will not be disturbed. The less vibration, the better.

> A very solid surface would be the poured concrete floor of a garage or basement.

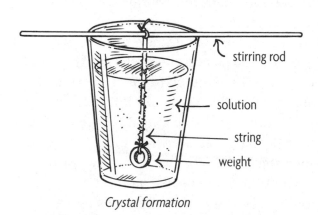

Crystal formation

8. As the solvent evaporates, crystals will form on the string. They become visible after several days. Some regularity to the crystal form should become evident. When the crystals are large and well formed, remove the string, allow it to dry, and sketch the crystals as they appear under the microscope or magnifying glass.

> The string provides a surface for the solute to crystallize on. Crystals tend to form around impurities and intrusions. Sometimes as solutions cool, the solutes remain dissolved beyond the quantity that would ordinarily dissolve. These solutions are called **supersaturated,** and a sudden disturbance or addition of a particle can trigger the solute to immediately **precipitate** (separate from the solution).

9. Repeat your experiment with other solids, such as sugar and salt. Compare your findings.

   a. How does the crystal form vary among the different solutes?

   b. How does their solubility compare?

> Sugar is much more soluble than salt. A saturated solution of sugar water will contain many times more sugar by weight than a saturated one of salt.

   c. How does their rate of crystallization compare? Compare the weight of different strings that have the same length and growing conditions.

References

Crystals and Crystal Gardens You Can Grow by Jean Stangl (Danbury, Conn.: Franklin Watts, 1990).

Crystals for Kids (Little Angel Books) by Leia A. Stinnett (Flagstaff, Ariz.: Light Technology Publications, 1997).

Grow Your Own Crystals (book and crystal kit) by David Packard (Mahwah, N.J.: Troll, 1995).

Non-Newtonian Fluids

Matter generally takes on one of three different **phases** (forms): solid, liquid, or gas. But did you ever play with Silly Putty?

> In a solid, atoms and molecules are in close, fixed positions, vibrating in place in a crystal structure. In a liquid, these particles are close together, too, but they move around at various speeds. Solids and liquids have definite volumes. In a gas, atoms and molecules are much farther apart, whizzing around space with no fixed volume.

What phase is it? Silly Putty is one of many substances that does not neatly fall into one phase category. Like slime and goop, Silly Putty shows elements of being both a solid and a liquid. These weird chemicals and mixtures are sometimes called **non-Newtonian fluids,** implying that they somehow do not obey the traditional laws of physics described by Isaac Newton (1642–1727). Newton, however, was a very wise man and probably would have enjoyed playing with Silly Putty and explaining its novel properties.

Materials

- Silly Putty
- safety goggles
- water
- metric measuring cup and spoons
- cornstarch
- pie tin
- food coloring
- small weights (such as steel washers or fishing weights)
- 2 small bowls

- Elmer's glue
- borax (available in supermarkets in the laundry detergent section)
- mixing spoon
- medium-size bowl
- 4 packages of unflavored gelatin
- glycerin (available at drugstores)
- muffin molds or shallow cups
- vegetable oil spray
- timer

> Liquids take the shape of whatever container they are in.

Procedure

Examine Silly Putty for both its solid and its liquid properties. First study it in its container. Notice it has flowed like water to fill the bottom of the container. The surface is flat. Press it gently. It yields because the molecules are not in fixed positions. Now pull the putty apart quickly, with as much force as you can. It snaps apart like a solid. Roll it together into a ball and throw it against the wall or floor. Again it behaves like an elastic solid, bouncing back. The warmer Silly Putty is, the more it behaves like a liquid; the colder it is, the more it behaves like a solid. Now put on your safety goggles and make your own putty, goop, and slime.

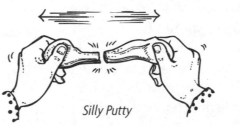

Silly Putty

To Make Cornstarch Putty

1. Mix warm water with cornstarch in a pie tin. Start with a small quantity of cornstarch—15 mL per 125 mL of water. Increase the amount of cornstarch 15 mL at a time to obtain different properties, each time mixing it in well and examining the result before adding more. You can make this and the other non-Newtonian fluids more colorful by adding a drop or two of food coloring.

2. Investigate how the putty's properties vary depending upon how you stress it. Pour it, hit it, cut it, and study its response to these actions.

3. You can do a quantitative study with small weights to see what the putty can support.

To Make Goop

1. In a small bowl, mix 350 mL of warm water, 475 mL of Elmer's glue, and a drop or two of food coloring. This is solution 1.

> The glue contains polyvinyl acetate molecules. The borax connects these molecules into long chains called **polymers.** Polymers are significant because of their great length and strength—polymers often twist around themselves like a tangled bundle of yarn.

2. In a second small bowl, mix 20 mL of borax (sodium borate), and 230 mL of warm water. This is solution 2.

3. Stir both solutions gently until they are uniform, then pour solution 1 into solution 2 without mixing or stirring. Your goop is done.

4. Test your goop. How does it differ from putty? Can a blob of goop support a small weight? If you pull the goop apart slowly, does it stretch like gum, or break like a solid? What if you pull it apart quickly? What happens when you twist it, first slowly and then quickly?

5. Wash your hands after handling the goop, as it can irritate your skin.

To Make Homemade Slime

1. In a medium-size bowl, mix four packages of unflavored gelatin with 200 mL of warm water. Add 25 mL of glycerin, and a drop or two of food coloring. Stir gently.

2. Spray some muffin molds or shallow cups with vegetable oil.

3. Add the slime to the molds and let it set for 20 minutes.

Slime

4. Remove the slime and handle it gently. How does slime differ from putty and goop?

References

Janice VanCleave's 200 Gooey, Slippery, Slimy, Weird, and Fun Experiments by Janice VanCleave (New York: John Wiley & Sons, 1993).

Kitchen Chemistry: Science Experiments to Do at Home by Robert Gardner, ed. Jane Steltenpohl (Parsippany, N.J.: Silver Burdett/Messner, 1989).

Science Experiments You Can Eat, rev. ed., by Vicki Cobb (New York: HarperCollins Children's Books, 1994).

Vicki Cobb's Kids' Science Page: www.vickicobb.com

20 Measuring the Thickness of an Oil Slick

"Oil and water don't mix." This common expression can be easily seen in salad dressing: the oil floats on top of the vinegar. Even when you shake the bottle, the vinegar remains together in cohesive

> **Cohesion** is the attraction between molecules of the same substance.

droplets spread throughout the oil. "Oil quiets troubled waters" is another expression that comes from a very interesting fact: if you pour a small amount of oil in a large body of water, the slick will spread evenly across the surface, reducing wave activity. About 40 cc of oil will calm more than 1 ha (hectare) of water. Oil, unlike water, does not cling to itself well, so the molecules spread out in a thin film instead of forming droplets. For many oils, the slick that forms is actually only one molecule thick. You can easily calculate this thickness.

> Benjamin Franklin observed the calming effects of oil on water in 1765. He wrote: "Where there is on the common a large pond which I observed one day to be very rough with the wind, I fetched out a cruet of oil and dropped a little of it on the water. I saw it spread itself with surprising swiftness upon the surface.... The oil, though not more than a teaspoonful, produced an instant calm over a space several yards square, which spread amazingly and extended itself gradually.... Making all that quarter of the pond, perhaps half an acre, as smooth as a looking glass."

Materials

- safety goggles
- oil samples (Regular olive oil works well. You can also use household oils, such as WD-40, lubricating oil, and furniture polish, to compare their different behaviors.)
- dropper pipette or paper clip
- paper towels
- metric ruler or meterstick
- child's wading pool or a large bathtub
- detergent
- water
- garden hose
- talcum powder (The unperfumed, unmedicated talcum powder used in hospitals works best.)
- notebook and pencil
- 8-cm stick of balsa wood
- utility scissors
- petroleum jelly
- gum camphor

Oils

Procedure

1. Put on your safety goggles and begin by practicing handling and measuring the oil. Use a dropper pipette or paper clip to make tiny droplets of oil. Practice dropping them on a paper towel. Measure them with a ruler. You want to make as small a measurable droplet as possible—1 to 2 mm is good.

2. Clean the wading pool or bathtub thoroughly with a few drops of detergent and a strong stream of water from a garden hose. The cleaner the better—you want to remove all residual oils from human skin and lotions.

> Thorough cleaning is essential. A flyspeck of contaminant can ruin your results.

3. Fill the pool or tub with clean water. When the water is calm, sprinkle a small amount of talcum powder over the center of the water. Use just enough of a dusting to see the powder form a small "cloud" at the surface of the water.

4. Measure the diameter of an oil droplet at the mouth of the pipette or the end of the paper clip. Gently drop it or

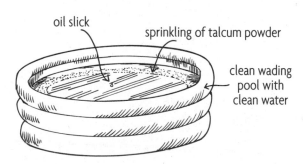

oil slick

sprinkling of talcum powder

clean wading pool with clean water

touch it into the center of the powder. The oil will rapidly spread over the surface, pushing the powder outward and forming a circle of oil.

5. As soon as the circle stops growing, measure the diameter.

6. Remove your safety goggles and calculate the thickness of the oil slick as follows. For oil monolayers (a **monolayer** is a layer one molecule thick), this is the thickness of individual molecules.

> To make an oil slick–powered boat, fashion a toy boat from a flat stick of balsa wood about 8 cm long. Cut the bow end (the front) to a point, and the stern end (the back) to a rectangular notch. Smear everything but the stern with white Vaseline or generic petroleum jelly. Press a small lump of gum camphor into the notch, and launch the boat in the pool or tub. The camphor molecules rushing from the stern will push the boat. If you put your finger to one side of the boat, the natural oils on your skin can exert enough pressure to steer the boat in the other direction.

Use the same units for all your measurements (e.g., millimeters).

a. Divide the diameter of the oil droplet by 2 to get r, the radius of the droplet.

b. Divide the diameter of the oil circle by 2 to get R, the radius of the oil slick.

c. Calculate the volume of the oil droplet. Use $V = 4/3(\pi r^3)$.

d. Calculate the area of the oil slick. Use $A = \pi R^2$.

e. Divide the volume by the area (V/A) to get t, the thickness. It's a *very* small value.

> π = approximately 3.14

> Sample thickness calculation: if $r = 1$ mm and $R = 1,200$ mm, then $t = 9.25 \times 10^{-7}$ mm, or approximately one millionth of a millimeter! The thickness of your oil slick depends on the type of oil you use—whether it forms monolayers, and how large the molecules are.

> Molecules are so small they are often measured in angstrom units. One **angstrom** is one ten-billionth of a meter.

References

After the Spill: The Exxon Valdez Disaster, Then and Now by Sandra Markle (New York: Walker, 1999).

Experiments That Explore Oil Spills by Martin Gutnik (Fresno, Calif.: Millbrook Press, 1991).

EARTH SCIENCE

21 Backyard Archaeology

You don't have to be Indiana Jones to find archaeological treasures, as long as you have the right tools, some patience, and an understanding of what can happen to human artifacts through years of burial. Your own neighborhood may contain buried arrowheads, antique glass, coins, and other items worthy of excavation and display. The most skilled archaeologists are very organized, work carefully, extract and handle their specimens gently, and keep thorough records of their work.

> You may be able to find arrowheads in areas once inhabited by American Indians. Old hunting sites and campgrounds are good places to look. Streambeds are, too—sometimes you can find an arrowhead among the gravel. Of course, you should have permission from the landowner to search for arrowheads or to remove them from his or her site.

Artifacts

Materials
- dig site
- map of the area
- metric ruler
- plant stakes (available at hardware or garden stores)
- string
- graph paper and pencil
- small shovel or spade
- spoon
- small, soft paintbrushes
- bowl of water and sponge
- notebook
- camera (optional)
- glue (optional)
- large box (optional)
- toothpicks or straws (optional)

Procedure

1. Choose a site for your archaeological dig. Your own backyard might be a good spot, but only if your house is considerably old—100 years or more. Some of the best places to dig include very old garbage piles and old farmyards. Always get permission from the owner before starting any dig.

2. Research the history of your area. Get as detailed a map as possible. Make use of state organizations and local historical societies. Who lived there, and when? What were their culture and society like? What can you find out about the geology and soil where you will be digging? What do you expect to find?

3. Divide the area you've chosen into a grid of 10-cm squares, using plant stakes and string as shown. Make a diagram of your archaeological dig site on graph paper, showing the stakes as dots and the strings as lines.

4. Start your dig carefully, working on one or two squares at a time. Work to depths of 10-cm intervals. Use a small shovel or spade or a spoon to remove soil gently and in small amounts, taking care not to damage anything you might find. Use a small paintbrush to remove soil from the extracted artifacts. Only if they look as if they can withstand water should you clean them gently in a bowl of water, using a sponge. Do not attempt to clean coins other than by brushing them with a soft paintbrush, since scratching them or using chemicals can decrease their value.

5. Log all your findings, keeping a careful record of where and how each item was obtained. Each specimen should be numbered and listed in a notebook very clearly so that anyone can readily identify it. You may also want to make sketches or take photographs of the objects found at the site.

6. You may wish to repair broken items with glue. Talk to your shop or technology teacher for restoration ideas.

7. You can re-create your dig site in an exhibit in school by using a large box, stakes and string, and your careful

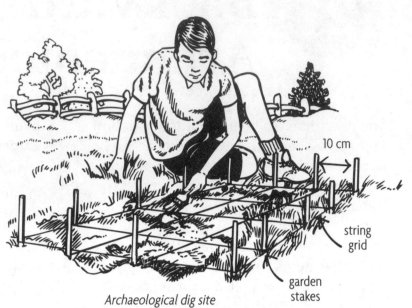

Archaeological dig site

10 cm

string grid

garden stakes

records. Or make a scale model of the site using toothpicks or straws for stakes, and sketches or photos of the objects.

8. If you think that you have an important find on your hands—like gold jewelry or a human skull—the next step is to tell your parents and teacher so they can help you get the assistance of local archaeologists and historians. You could donate your treasures to a museum and become a local legend!

References

Adventures in Archaeology (Scientific American Sourcebooks) by Tom McGowen (Chicago: Twenty-First Century Books, 1997).

The Archaeology Kit: Science Action Book (book and kit) by Ingrid Cranfield (Philadelphia: Running Press, 1998).

Archaeology Smart Junior: Discovering History's Buried Treasures by Karen Laubenstein and Ronald Roy (New York: Princeton Review, 1997).

Archeology (Eyewitness Books) by Jane McIntosh (New York: Knopf, 1994).

22 Building a Rock and Mineral Collection

Minerals are inorganic natural substances containing one or more elements.

Rocks are mixtures of minerals blended and bonded by ancient geological processes.

> Sandstone is a sedimentary rock. **Sedimentary rocks** are formed from the buildup of sediments deposited on riverbeds and ocean floors, and often contain fossils. Marble is a metamorphic rock. **Metamorphic rocks** are altered by heat and pressure deep in Earth's crust, and often have light and dark bands. Obsidian is an igneous rock. **Igneous rocks** are produced when **magma** (molten rock beneath Earth's surface) reaches the surface through volcanoes, flows as lava, and cools. Obsidian, a natural form of glass, is smooth and shiny.

You can easily build a rock and mineral collection with samples gathered from your yard and neighborhood, and from trips to other places. You can also add specimens purchased in science stores and gift shops, many of which are available for a dollar or less. As you study your samples, you will fill in important information about each sample, much as a detective solves a mystery. After determining the physical properties of a sample, you will be able use to your field guide and try to identify it.

Materials

- mineral and rock samples
- pencil, paper, and metric ruler
- mineral hardness kit (You can purchase a mineral hardness kit, or create your own kit with samples of the following minerals: talc, gypsum, calcite, fluorite, apatite, orthoclase, quartz, topaz, corundum, diamond; or use a pin, a knife, and a piece of glass.)
- white, unglazed piece of tile to use as a streak plate (The back of a spare ceramic bathroom or kitchen tile works well.)
- safety goggles
- hammer and anvil, or bench vise
- electronic or pan balance, or postal scale
- graduated cylinder wide enough for the sample to fit into (A small measuring cup or a rain gauge with milliliter markings can be used in place of a graduated cylinder.)
- water
- directional compass (optional)
- ultraviolet light (optional)
- rock and mineral field guide
- local geology guide (from your bookstore or library)
- clear plastic display box (optional)

Procedure

1. Spread out your mineral and rock samples on a work surface.

2. Use a pencil, paper, and ruler to create a table like the one shown (the first row is completed as an example).

Mineral	Origin	Hardness	Streak	Cleavage (crystal system)	Specific gravity	Notes
Quartz	Underhill quarry	7.0	colorless	hexagonal	2.65	Contains some impurities

3. Begin by filling in the origin of your first sample—where you found it. Be as specific as possible about location and position.

4. The first property to measure is mineral hardness. Test each sample using your mineral hardness kit and the following mineral hardness scale (Mohs' scale). According to **Mohs' scale,** any mineral can be scratched by a mineral of greater hardness.

Mohs' Scale

1. talc (crushes easily between fingers, feels powdery)

2. gypsum (can be scratched with a finger-nail)

3. calcite (can be scratched with a pin)

4. fluorite (can be scratched with a knife blade)

5. apatite (hard to scratch with a knife)

6. orthoclase (can be used to scratch a knife)

7. quartz (will scratch glass)

8. topaz

9. corundum

10. diamond

To determine where the mineral falls on the scale, test its hardness against the known samples in your kit. For instance, if a mineral can be scratched with a knife blade but not with a pin, record the hardness as 3.5, since it is between 3 and 4 on the hardness scale. A mineral can scratch any mineral with a lesser hardness value, and can be scratched by any mineral with a greater hardness value.

5. Next, determine the **streak** by rubbing the mineral against a streak plate to see what color it leaves behind. Note whether the streak is colorless, white, gray, or another color.

unglazed back of bathroom tile
Streak plate and mineral samples

6. **Cleavage** is the tendency of a mineral to break in the direction of its crystal system (see chapter 18, "Growing Crystals"). You can often determine the cleavage just by looking at the sample. Quartz is a hexagonal crystal, with six sides. Halite is cubic, with four sides. Mica breaks into thin sheets. If you have extra samples of a rock or mineral, you can put on your safety gog-

quartz (hexagonal—6 sides)

halite (cubic—cubes on cubes)

mica (thin sheets)

Cleavage of mineral samples

gles and break them with a hammer and anvil (or crush it in a vise) to see how they split.

7. The **specific gravity** can be found by calculating the sample's **density** (D), which is the ratio of mass (m) to volume (V). ($D = m/V$). First, measure the mass of your sample in grams with an electronic balance. You can use a home office postal scale and multiply ounces by 28 to get grams. Next, fill a graduated cylinder halfway with water and note how much the liquid rises when you drop the rock in it. For instance, if the water rises from 5.0 mL to 7.2 mL, the volume of the rock is the difference, 2.2 mL. If you are using a measuring cup with ounces, you can convert ounces to milliliters by multiplying by 28. Finally, divide the mass by the volume. Use the number you get as the specific gravity—how much denser your rock is than water.

8. Note any other special properties your sample has, using your senses and other equipment you might have at your disposal. Does it feel greasy? Does it have a distinct odor? Is your mineral magnetic? If so, it will affect the needle on a compass. Will it glow under ultra-violet (black) light? If so, it is phosphorescent. **Phosphorescence** is the process by which a substance absorbs electromagnetic radiation at one wavelength and then releases it over time at another, as glow-in-the-dark materials do.

> Magnetite will attract iron filings and move a compass needle. Franklinite glows eerily under UV light. Sulfur smells like rotten eggs.

9. Use a good rock and mineral field guide and a local roadside geology book for the region where you live to identify the samples in your collection. You can purchase a clear plastic display box with compartments in hobby and craft stores, and label your collection for display. Add to your collection when you travel to distant places.

References

A Field Guide to Rocks and Minerals, 5th ed. (Peterson Field Guides) by Frederick H. Pough and Roger Tory Peterson (Boston: Houghton Mifflin, 1998).

Rocks and Minerals (Eyewitness Books) by R. F. Symes (Topeka, Kans.: Econo-Clad Books, 1999).

23 Fossil Models

Fossils are formed in several different ways. Sometimes actual animal and plant remains are trapped in a substance and preserved, as are ants in amber (fossilized tree sap) and woolly mammoths in ice.

> Woolly mammoths lived during the last ice age. Although they are now extinct, people sometimes find their frozen bodies in far northern latitudes.

Sometimes minerals may replace the remains, leaving a hard replica, as happens when petrified wood forms. **Trace fossils** are imprints of plants and creatures on surrounding material, such as footprints that have hardened into rock. The original remains are gone, but you can see where the fossil was: a three-dimensional imprint of past life.

> The coelacanth, a rare fish once thought to be extinct, is called a "living fossil" because it bears such striking similarity to fossils that formed millions of years ago.

insect in amber

dinosaur footprint

Fossils

You can build models of fossils using common materials. If you live or travel to the right geographic area, you can find and collect real fossils, or you can purchase fossils from some museum or fossil stores.

Materials

- nut, seed, or other natural object
- artist's paintbrushes
- floor wax
- plaster of paris
- water
- shallow dish
- silicone caulking gel
- paint
- fossil field guide

Procedure

To Make the Mold

1. Select a natural object from which to make a model trace fossil, such as a nut or a seed.

2. Clean the surface of the object with a paintbrush.

3. Use a paintbrush to coat the object with floor wax, to make later extraction easy.

4. Mix some plaster of paris according to the package instructions.

5. Put the plaster into a shallow dish and rest the object in it. To make extraction easy, do not immerse the object completely.

6. Allow the plaster to harden overnight.

7. Extract the object from the plaster. You have made a **mold** of the object.

object coated with floor wax

shallow bowl with plaster of paris

Making a mold

To Make the Model Fossil

1. Fill the mold with silicone gel, and allow the gel to harden.

2. Extract the hardened gel gently with your fingers. This is the **cast** and should look much like your original object. Paint the cast for display.

Impressions are the images left by plant or animal remains after they have been pressed against sediment such as clay or soil. If remnants of the original organism remain, the remains are called a **compression.**

References

Animals Dazzlers: The World of Animal Fossils by Collard B. Sneed III (Danbury, Conn.: Franklin Watts, 1999).

Death Trap: The Story of the La Brea Tar Pits by Sharon Elaine Thompson (Minneapolis: Lerner, 1994).

Fossils (Dorling Kindersley Pocket series) by Douglas Palmer (New York: Dorling Kindersley, 1996).

If You Are a Hunter of Fossils by Byrd Baylor (New York: Aladdin Paperbacks, 1984).

Is There a Dinosaur in Your Backyard? The World's Most Fascinating Fossils, Rocks, and Minerals by Spencer Christian and Antonia Felix (New York: John Wiley & Sons, 1998).

Fossils—Behind the Scenes at the Royal Ontario Museum:
www.rom.on.ca/quiz/fossil/

Fossils—Windows to the Past:
www.ucmp.berkeley.edu/paleo/fossils/permin.html

You can successfully find fossils in certain geographic areas. Get a fossil field guide from a bookstore or library to conduct your search. The following are just a few examples of fruitful fossil locations:

- Portland, Connecticut: Dinosaur footprints in brownstone.
- Deschutes River, Oregon: Petrified wood along the riverbanks.
- San Pedro, California: Head of a Miocene baleen whale found in stone.
- Cook County, Illinois: Sea-dwelling creatures fossilized in Niagara limestone.
- The American Museum of Natural History in New York, of course! Museums are the best place of all to find fossils.

You can bring your materials to these locations and make plaster molds to take imprints of fossils in the stone. Of course, you should always have permission from landowners before entering their property or conducting archaeological work there. You are generally not allowed to take fossils from public lands.

Clouds are concentrations of water vapor in the sky. They form when water **evaporates** (turns to water vapor) from oceans and freshwater sources, such as ponds and lakes. As the water vapor swirls around, it **condenses** (changes to a liquid) and forms small droplets, which in turn, bump into each other and join to form larger droplets. This results in **precipitation,** especially if the vapor cloud encounters a mass of cold air. Water falls to earth as liquid droplets or ice crystals—rain, sleet, hail, or snow—depending upon the air conditions. A typical raindrop is 0.1 mm in diameter, although it could easily be larger or smaller.

Cirrus clouds are high, white, and wispy. **Stratus clouds** are gray and hover close to the ground in layers. Cirrus and stratus clouds often bring light precipitation and fog. (At altitudes over 15 m, fog is considered to be a cloud.) **Cumulus clouds** look like white tufts of cotton candy and usually accompany fair weather. **Cumulonimbus clouds** are huge black clouds that often lead to lightning, thunder, and heavy rain. **Nimbus clouds** are low, dark clouds that lead to rain or snow.

The conditions that lead to cloud formation are easy to reproduce on a small scale. You can condense water vapor into liquid droplets to model what happens in the sky overhead. This activity has two parts: making little clouds, and condensing them into miniature rainstorms.

Materials

- water
- beaker (or heat-resistant Pyrex or Kimax cup)
- stove or hot plate (*requires adult help*)
- tongs or thick oven mitt
- timer
- metric measuring spoons
- Erlenmeyer flask (A narrow-mouthed bottle will do.)
- ice
- clamp and support (optional)
- metal pan (such as a pie tin or cake pan)
- metric ruler
- cup
- notebook and pencil

Procedure

To Make Clouds

1. Have an adult help you heat water in a half-filled beaker until it boils, and set it to the side using tongs or a thick oven mitt. Let the water cool for 30 seconds to 1 minute.

2. Use the tongs to pour a small amount of the hot water 20 to 30 mL—into a flask.

3. Place an ice cube so that it rests on the mouth of the flask. (If necessary, fuse a couple of cubes by squeezing them together, to prevent them from falling into the flask).

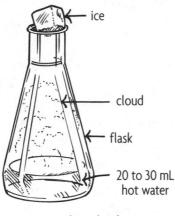

Making clouds

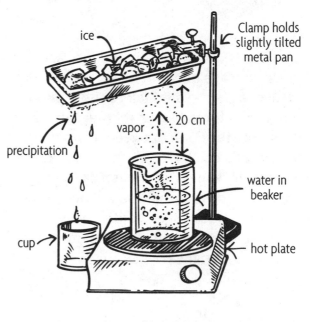

Making rain

4. Observe what happens inside the flask.

5. As an extension, vary the initial temperature of the water, or the amount of ice, to compare the rate and quality of cloud formation.

To Make Rain

1. Adjust the amount of water in the beaker so that it is half full. Set the beaker on a hot plate.

2. Using a clamp, mount a metal pan to a support 10 to 20 cm above the beaker, at a slight angle. Put enough ice cubes in the pan to cover the bottom. (If you do not have the equipment to clamp the pan in place, you can ask an adult to hold the pan by the edge using an oven mitt. Make sure the person keeps his or her hand away from the steam.)

3. Have an adult bring the water in the beaker to a boil.

4. Observe what happens on the bottom of the metal pan. Collect the "precipitation" that drips off the pan in a cup.

5. You may also want to measure and record variables such as the length of time the water boils, the volume of the water that boils off, and the volume of precipitation that falls.

References

Clouds: From Mare's Tails to Thunderheads (First Book series) by Suzanne Harper (Danbury, Conn.: Franklin Watts, 1997).

Janice VanCleave's Weather: Mind-Boggling Experiments You Can Turn into Science Fair Projects (Spectacular Science Projects series) by Janice VanCleave (New York: John Wiley & Sons, 1995).

Science Projects about Weather (Science Projects series) by Robert Gardner and David Webster (Berkeley Heights, N.J.: Enslow, 1994).

Simple Weather Experiments with Everyday Materials by Muriel Mandell (New York: Sterling, 1991).

Measuring Raindrops

Precipitation can take many forms. Rain is mostly drops of liquid water, which condense in the sky and fall to the ground under the force of **gravity** (a weak mutual force of attraction between all matter). Raindrops can be big, like a pencil eraser, or tiny, forming a light mist. Factors that affect raindrop formation include air temperature, wind speed, and air pressure. You can capture and study raindrops with simple materials.

Materials

- solid metal block (A rectangular block of iron 2 by 10 by 20 cm is ideal. If you have a small anvil, it will work fine.)
- spray oil (must be an organic compound. Organic compounds contain carbon. You can use cooking spray, WD-40, or spot remover.)
- freezer
- timer
- metric ruler or meterstick
- assorted droppers or pipettes with bulbs
- water
- graduated cylinder
- notebook and pencil
- graph paper
- safe balcony (*requires adult permission*)

Procedure

1. Spray a solid metal block lightly with oil. Give the block a *very* light coating—not enough to bead or run off.

2. Place your block in a freezer for 1 hour per centimeter of thickness.

3. Your droppers (or pipettes) should dispense a variety of droplet sizes. The narrower the dropper, the smaller the droplets. Choose a dropper and follow these steps to determine the volume of each drop that it dispenses.

   a. Give the mouth of the dropper a quick, light spray of oil.

   > By oiling a surface, the water tends not to stick to it. Chemists have an expression "like dissolves like." It means that substances that are similar in nature, such as two organic liquids, dissolve in each other. Water and oil will not dissolve in each other because water is polar (its molecules have an equal charge at each end—positive at the hydrogen atoms and negative at the oxygen atom) and oil is not.

   b. Determine how many drops of water it takes to fill the graduated cylinder to a volume of 1 mL.

   c. Divide 1 mL by the number of drops to get the volume of each drop.

   > For example, if your dropper produces 28 drops per milliliter, the volume of each drop is 1.0 mL/28 drops = 0.0357 mL/drop.

   d. Repeat this calculation for the other droppers you have available.

4. Remove the block from the freezer, place it on the floor, and follow these steps to study the relationship between a drop's volume and the diameter of its resulting splash pattern.

a. Release a drop from a position exactly 1 m above the block. Make an effort to hold the dropper still and squeeze it gently until the drop is released. It will hit the block, spread out, and freeze onto the cold surface. Measure and record the diameter of the frozen splash pattern.

> Freezing water undergoes a **phase change** from liquid to solid. Heat flows from the liquid and enters the block.

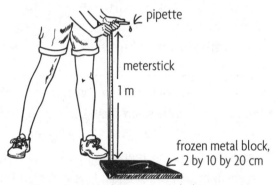

Dropping water to create a splash pattern

b. Repeat with the other droppers, each time ensuring that the drop falls from the same height.

c. Graph the splash pattern diameter as a function of the drop volume.

5. Study the relationship between height of release and the splash pattern diameter.

> Chances are your graph will not be linear or proportional. This is because the volume of the splash pattern increases directly with the square of the diameter. For instance, a splash pattern 2 cm in diameter has four times the area of one that is 1 cm in diameter. This is because the formula for the area of a circle is $A = \pi r2$.

a. Select just one dropper, and vary the height from which you release the drops.

b. Release drops from successively doubling heights, such as 10 cm, 20 cm, 40 cm, 80 cm, and so on.

c. Graph the splash pattern diameter as a function of height. Regions of your graph should be linear, indicating a proportion.

6. Use your data to study real raindrops.

a. Repeat step 4, releasing the drops from a safe balcony—5 m or higher—and graphing the splash pattern diameter.

b. During a rainstorm, put your metal block outside and capture a dozen or so raindrops. Measure their splash patterns.

c. Use your graph from step 6a to figure out the original volume of each raindrop. Assume the raindrops fell at the same speed as the ones you released from the balcony.

References

Can It Really Rain Frogs? The World's Strangest Weather Events (Spencer Christian's World of Wonders series) by Spencer Christian and Antonia Felix (New York: John Wiley & Sons, 1997).

University of Michigan Weather Underground: groundhog.sprl.umich.edu/index.html

USA Today weather: www.usatoday.com/weather/wfront.htm

The Weather Channel home page: www.weather.com/twc/homepage.twc

When you step out of a swimming pool in the summer, you feel much cooler than before you jumped in. This is because you are wet, and the heat of the air causes evaporation to take place at your skin's surface. The water molecules on your skin are moving at different speeds. The heated molecules on the surface move faster, have more energy, and escape (evaporate) into the air. Your internal heat moves to the surface to replace the energy, so your body cools off. This is also why sweating cools you down. Similarly, a wet thermometer will record a lower temperature as it dries than a dry thermometer. Using this principle, you can measure the humidity of the air. All you need are some basic materials and a conversion table.

> **Relative humidity** is a measure of the amount of water in the air, as compared to the greatest possible amount that the air could hold at that temperature. A comfortable humidity level is approximately 50 to 70 percent. Ten percent would be a typical reading in the desert, which can feel very dry; 90 percent on a hot day in the summer in the city makes for unpleasant conditions. Humidity is measured with a **hygrometer** (not to be confused with a **hydrometer,** which measures either the density or the specific gravity of a liquid.)

Materials

- red-alcohol Celsius thermometer with exposed bulb
- timer
- notebook and pencil
- scissors
- cotton gauze (available at pharmacies)
- small rubber band
- bowl of water
- small fan or twine
- meterstick
- safety goggles (if using twine)

Procedure

1. Allow a thermometer to adjust to the external air temperature for 3 minutes. Record the temperature. This is the dry-bulb temperature.

> The red alcohol in the thermometer expands when heated and contracts when cooled, moving up and down a narrow glass tube. This is how liquid thermometers work. Some thermometers have silvery mercury in them, but you should avoid using these types because mercury is toxic and if the thermometer breaks, you will cause dangerous mercury contamination in the room.

2. Cut a narrow piece of gauze and wrap it around the thermometer bulb, and fasten it with a rubber band. Dip the bulb in a bowl of water briefly to wet it. Hold the thermometer bulb in front of a fan turned on to high and hold the thermometer in the blowing air for approximately 1 minute.

> You can use a small electric fan—the handheld ones that use batteries work well. You can even use a paper or cardboard fan, if you move it briskly with your hand.

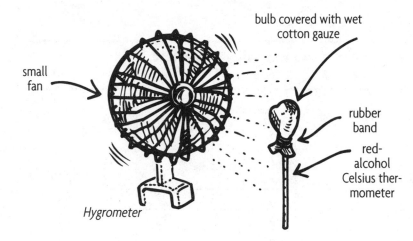

small fan

bulb covered with wet cotton gauze

rubber band

red-alcohol Celsius thermometer

Hygrometer

Instead of using a fan, you can make a **sling psychrometer** (a device that measures relative humidity by comparing wet-bulb and dry-bulb temperatures). Tie the thermometer securely to 1 m of twine, put on safety goggles, and swing it in a circular motion for up to 1 minute. This has the same effect as the fan: air rushes over the bulb, cooling off the thermometer.

Record the lowest temperature that the thermometer attains. This is the wet-bulb temperature.

3. Subtract the wet-bulb temperature from the dry-bulb temperature and record the difference.

4. Using the values you obtained in steps 1 and 3, and the table on the following page, determine the relative humidity in the air. Now you know what the meteorologists mean when they give the relative humidity.

5. To make a more formal study, you can compare the relative humidity in different locations. For instance, how does the humidity compare inside your bedroom; in the bathroom, before and after taking a shower; in the kitchen while preparing food; outside; in your basement; in your attic; in your garage; at the edge of a pond; in the middle of a parking lot?

On hot, humid days, you feel sticky because the air already has a lot of water in it; therefore, your perspiration does not evaporate easily.

6. Alternatively, you can record the humidity over a 2-week period from one location near your home. Compare your findings to weather reports. When the wind blows in from the ocean or a large lake, you should see a rise in humidity; if it comes from inland, or has passed over a mountain range, you can expect the weather to be drier (lower humidity). Using a hydrometer, and with some practice, you can predict the weather with reliability.

References

Can It Really Rain Frogs? The World's Strangest Weather Events (Spencer Christian's World of Wonders series) by Spencer Christian and Antonia Felix (New York: John Wiley & Sons, 1997).

It's Raining Cats and Dogs: All Kinds of Weather, and Why We Have It by Franklyn Mansfield Branley (New York: Morrow/Avon, 1993).

"Waiter, There's a Hair in My Hygrometer" by Shawn Carlson: www.sciam.com/1998/0698issue/0698amsci.html

Weather (Eyewitness Explorers Series) by John Farndon and John Bendall-Brunello (New York: Dorling Kindersley, 1992).

RELATIVE HUMIDITY CONVERSION TABLE

Dry-bulb temperature	Dry-bulb temperature minus wet-bulb temperature, °C									
	1	2	3	4	5	6	7	8	9	10
10°C	88	77	66	55	44	34	24	15	6	
11°C	89	78	67	56	46	36	27	18	9	
12°C	89	78	68	58	48	39	29	21	12	
13°C	89	79	69	59	50	41	32	22	15	7
14°C	90	79	70	60	51	42	34	26	18	10
15°C	90	80	71	61	53	44	36	27	20	13
16°C	90	81	71	63	54	46	38	30	23	15
17°C	90	81	72	64	55	47	40	32	25	18
18°C	91	82	73	65	57	49	41	34	27	20
19°C	91	82	74	65	58	40	43	36	29	22
20°C	91	83	74	66	59	51	44	37	31	24
21°C	91	83	75	67	60	53	46	39	32	26
22°C	92	83	76	68	61	54	47	40	34	28
23°C	92	84	76	69	62	55	48	42	36	30
24°C	92	84	77	69	62	56	49	43	37	31
25°C	92	84	77	70	63	57	50	44	39	33
26°C	92	85	78	71	64	58	51	46	40	34
27°C	92	85	78	71	65	58	52	47	41	36
28°C	93	85	78	72	65	59	53	48	42	37
29°C	93	86	79	72	66	60	54	49	43	38
30°C	93	86	79	73	67	61	55	50	44	39

27 Building an Anemometer

Wind speed is an important quantity for meteorologists to measure when they report and predict the weather. They use a device called an **anemometer** to measure wind speed. Although some anemometers are expensive, sophisticated electronic devices, it is easy to build an inexpensive and fairly accurate one using string and a table-tennis ball.

> Another way to make an anemometer is to put a small windmill on an electric generator. The output of the generator varies with the velocity of the windmill and is measured by a meter attached to the generator.

Materials

- table-tennis (Ping-Pong) ball
- sewing needle
- thin fishing line (A typical rating would be 0.08 mm and 0.011 g/m. Monofilament sewing thread will also work if it has a diameter of 0.2 mm or less.)
- plastic cement
- scissors
- plastic protractor
- metric ruler
- spirit level
- 40-cm wooden dowel
- electric drill and bit (*requires adult help*)
- small screw and screwdriver
- notebook and pencil

> Table-tennis balls are ideal because they must meet rigid specifications of diameter and weight. Table-tennis balls meet specifications set by the International Table Tennis Federation. The median diameter of 37.7 mm may vary by no more than 1.3 percent, and the weight of 2.465 g by no more than 2.56 percent.

Procedure

1. Pierce the ball with a needle at two opposite points. The perforations may produce two shallow indentations. Use the needle to thread the fishing line through the ball. Fasten one end of the line to the ball with a dab of plastic cement. (Use cement that does not dissolve the ball chemically.) After the cement has hardened, trim the surplus bit of line as close as possible to the ball's surface.

2. Pass the free end of the line through the index hole of an ordinary plastic protractor. The protractor serves as the scale for measuring the angular deflection (tilt) of the hanging ball with respect to the horizontal tilt. Adjust the length of line between the upper surface of the ball and the index hole of the protractor to 30 cm and attach the free end of the line to the rear surface of the protractor with cement as shown.

3. Cement an ordinary spirit level parallel to and near the baseline of the protractor.

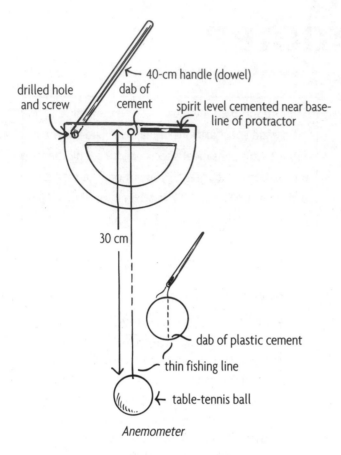

drilled hole and screw

40-cm handle (dowel)

dab of cement

spirit level cemented near base-line of protractor

30 cm

dab of plastic cement

thin fishing line

table-tennis ball

Anemometer

away from your body, and level as indicated by the air bubble in the spirit level. (The air bubble should rest between the hairlines.) Note the angle that the fishing line crosses on the protractor. Find the corresponding wind speed using the table provided. For instance, an angle of 60 degrees indicates a wind speed of 6.66 m per second. Use other data you collect, such as temperature and relative humidity, to predict the weather. (See chapter 26, "Making a Hygrometer," for information on determining relative humidity.)

4. Fashion a handle from a 40-cm dowel. The handle will allow you to hold the instrument away from your body. If you hold the instrument away from your body and stay out of the path of the wind (don't stand downwind of the instrument), your body will not change the wind speed you are trying to measure. Ask an adult to drill a pilot hole for a screw in the protractor as shown. Screw the handle into the hole.

5. Go outside in an open area on a day when the wind is fairly noticeable. Hold the anemometer as still as possible,

The basic principle of the anemometer dates back at least to the fifteenth century. The anemometer designed for this experiment was calibrated in a wind tunnel. (For information on wind tunnels, see chapter 29, "Experiments in a Wind Tunnel.") Calibration is the process by which a measuring instrument is adjusted or interpreted to read accurately. If you make an exact copy of the instrument described here, you can expect it to produce reliable readings.

References

Rain, Wind, and Storm (Living with the Weather) by Nicola Baxter (Orlando, Fla.: Raintree/Steck-Vaughn, 1998).

The Wind at Work: An Activity Guide to Windmills by Gretchen Woelfle (Chicago: Chicago Review Press, 1997).

WIND SPEED CONVERSION TABLE

Angle	Miles per hour	Meters per second
20	32.5	14.5
21	31.6	14.1
22	30.8	13.8
23	30.1	13.5
24	29.4	13.1
25	28.7	12.8
26	28.1	12.5
27	27.5	12.3
28	26.9	12
29	26.3	11.8
30	25.8	11.5
31	25.3	11.3
32	24.8	11.1
33	24.3	10.9
34	23.9	10.7
35	23.4	10.5
36	23	10.3
37	22.6	10.1
38	22.2	9.91
39	21.8	9.74
40	21.4	9.57
41	21	9.40
42	20.7	9.24
43	20.3	9.08
44	19.9	8.92
45	19.6	8.76
46	19.3	8.61
47	18.9	8.46
48	18.6	8.32
49	18.3	8.17
50	18	8.03
51	17.6	7.89
52	17.3	7.75
53	17	7.61
54	16.7	7.47
55	16.4	7.33

Angle	Miles per hour	Meters per second
56	16.1	7.20
57	15.8	7.06
58	15.5	6.93
59	15.2	6.79
60	14.9	6.66
61	14.6	6.52
62	14.3	6.39
63	14	6.26
64	13.7	6.12
65	13.4	5.98
66	13.1	5.85
67	12.8	5.71
68	12.5	5.57
69	12.1	5.43
70	11.8	5.29
71	11.5	5.14
72	11.2	5
73	10.8	4.85
74	10.5	4.69
75	10.1	4.54
76	9.79	4.38
77	9.42	4.21
78	9.04	4.04
79	8.64	3.86
80	8.23	3.68
81	7.80	3.49
82	7.35	3.29
83	6.87	3.07
84	6.36	2.84
85	5.80	2.59
86	5.18	2.32
87	4.49	2.01
88	3.66	1.64
89	2.59	1.16
90	0	0

Earth Science
28 The Coriolis Effect

The **Coriolis force** comes from the rotation of Earth. Earth spins on its axis at a rate of one rotation per 24 hours. At the equator, this is equivalent to approximately 1,600 km per hour—this is the speed a person standing at the equator experiences. But at the North and South Poles, the speed is zero. This differential in speed causes eddies (swirling patterns) in the atmosphere. These in turn affect weather patterns.

> Put a few drops of food coloring on a tennis ball, gently lower it into a tub of water, and give it a spin with your fingers. Note the patterns of motion that the food coloring makes in the water.

Hurricanes spin counterclockwise in the Northern Hemisphere and clockwise in the Southern Hemisphere because of the Coriolis force.

> We don't notice the spinning of Earth directly, because we move at constant **velocity** (speed and direction).

> A popular myth holds that the water in toilets and sinks demonstrates the **Coriolis effect** (the observed effect of the Coriolis force) by draining counterclockwise in the Northern Hemisphere and clockwise in the Southern Hemisphere. However, this actually has to do with the design of the toilet or sink rather than where it is located on Earth.

NASA scientists must take Coriolis effects into consideration when they launch rockets. In fact, space launching facilities, including the Johnson Space Center in Houston and Cape Canaveral in Florida, are located in the south to take advantage of the greater speed of Earth's surface at those **latitudes** (distances north or south of the equator, measured by imaginary lines running east to west parallel to the equator). This activity shows you several ways to demonstrate the Coriolis force and its effects.

Materials

- 2-L soda bottle
- water
- food coloring
- metric ruler
- merry-go-round or a swivel chair and weights
- safety goggles
- steel washer, nut, or other small weight
- 1-m nylon fishing string or line

> These effects were first described by Gaspard-Gustave de Coriolis (1792–1843), a French engineer and mathematician.

Procedure

1. Fill a 2-L soda bottle with water. Turn it upside down and let the bottle begin to pour out. Swirl the bottle clockwise until a miniature cyclone starts. Study the cyclone as the water pours out. Notice that the swirl will remain powered by gravity even if you hold the bottle still. For a more dramatic effect, first release a drop of food coloring from a height of 10 cm and allow it to settle into the water. As an extension,

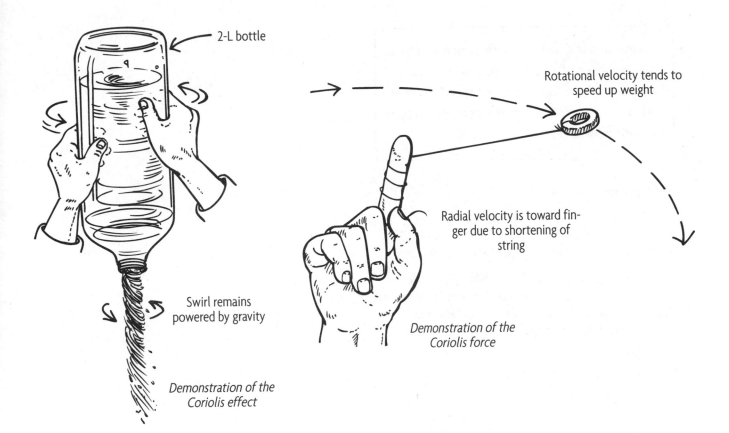

2-L bottle

Rotational velocity tends to speed up weight

Radial velocity is toward finger due to shortening of string

Swirl remains powered by gravity

Demonstration of the Coriolis effect

Demonstration of the Coriolis force

you can vary bottle sizes and mouth openings to find out what conditions work best to support this motion.

2. Get on a small merry-go-round and give it a good spin. Move toward the center. Notice what happens to the rate of rotation. You spin faster because of a principle called the conservation of angular momentum.

> **Angular momentum** is a quantity that is based upon an object's mass and rate of rotation.

Move back to the edge and the spinning slows down. You can demonstrate the same effect in a swivel chair by holding weights in your arms, spinning, and then moving your arms toward and away from your body, or by observing

figure skaters as they change their rate of rotation using their arms.

3. Put on your safety goggles, and swing a small weight in a circular orbit at the end of a 1-m string. Let the string wind around your finger as shown. The result is always the same—as the length of the string decreases, the speed of the weight increases. The string may be compared to a nearly massless merry-go-round and the weight to a heavy person.

> In physics terms, the weight has a **radial velocity** (speed of rotation in respect to angle) toward your finger because of the shortening of the string. The radial velocity interacts with the **rotational velocity** (the speed and direction the weight turns) to produce an acceleration that is **tangential** (touching but not intersecting) to the path of the weight and acts to speed up the weight.

As artificial satellites fall toward Earth out of their orbit, the radius of their orbit (the distance to Earth's center) decreases and their speed increases, until friction becomes so great that they burn up in the atmosphere.

References

Rocket Science: 50 Flying, Floating, Flipping, Spinning Gadgets Kids Create Themselves by Jim Wiese (New York: John Wiley & Sons, 1995).

The Spinning Blackboard and Other Dynamic Experiments on Force and Motion (Exploratorium Science Snackbook series) by Paul Doherty (New York: John Wiley & Sons, 1996).

PHYSICS

Experiments in a Wind Tunnel

The Swiss mathematician-scientist Daniel Bernoulli (1700–1782) is famous for discovering that as the speed of a liquid or gas increases, its pressure decreases. This is known as **Bernoulli's principle,** and it is the scientific foundation of modern airplane flight. The wing of a modern aircraft is rounded at the top. This increases the distance that the rushing air must travel relative to the lower edge of the wing. The air must move faster over the top of the wing than at the bottom, so there is lower pressure on top of the wing. The greater air pressure from below causes an upward force called **lift,** which lifts the wing—and the plane with it.

> If you hang two strips of paper parallel to each other and blow between them, they will move together. This works with hanging balloons as well. By blowing between the paper or balloons, you increase the speed of the air in between, causing the air pressure to decrease. The higher air pressure on the outside of each piece of paper or balloon pushes the object inward.

A **wind tunnel** is a device used to study the **aerodynamics** (airflow across surfaces) of objects. You can build a simple

> Orville Wright (1871–1948) took off on the world's first human flight on December 17, 1903, at Kitty Hawk, North Carolina. He would not have gotten very far if he and his brother had not done wind tunnel tests.

wind tunnel and conduct engineering tests on model planes and **airfoils** (wing samples).

Materials

- heavy cardboard box (such as one in which a computer has been shipped)
- pencil
- safety razor (*requires adult help*)
- air-conditioning filter or thin foam pad
- duct tape
- Plexiglas or clear plastic sheet, same size as largest wall of box
- electric fan (small enough to fit in one end of the box)
- balsa wood, hard packaging foam, or cardboard
- glue
- digital postal scale
- notebook
- different shaped objects, paper airplanes, model airplanes

Procedure

1. Construct the shell of your wind tunnel out of a cardboard box: Mark the cutting lines on the cardboard with a pencil first, then have an adult cut the sections out using a razor with a safety handle. Both ends of the box should be open. Divide the box into two unequal compartments by mounting an air-conditioning filter, secured with duct

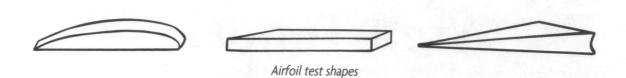

Airfoil test shapes

tape, approximately one-third of the way in from one end. The purpose of the filter is to help even out the airflow. Make a window in one side of the larger compartment, leaving a 2-cm border. Insert a sheet of Plexiglas inside the border to serve as a window pane, and secure it with duct tape.

2. Place a fan in the smaller compartment so that air blows through the filter into the larger compartment.

> Balloons do not rely upon Bernoulli's principle for aerodynamic lift. They rise because the internal gas—helium or hot air—is less dense than the surrounding atmosphere.

3. Make a variety of airfoils in the test shapes shown above, using balsa wood and glue. If balsa is not available, you can use hard packaging foam or cardboard. If you can, visit an airport and study the wing shapes on aircraft.

4. Mount one of your airfoil samples on the postal scale. Since the scale measures downward force, mount your sample upside down for purposes of gathering lift data. Tape the sample down using duct tape, with a small balsa cube separator holding it above the surface of the scale. (Tape the balsa cube to the scale.) The purpose of the separator is to allow airflow both above and below the airfoil. Keep in mind that when you place the scale in step 5, the front of the airfoil (or plane) should face the fan and the readout on the scale should face the open end of the wind tunnel.

5. Make sure the postal scale is set to measure weight (grams), not dollar postage values, then place it in the larger compartment.

6. Read the scale, then turn the fan on and read the scale again after a few seconds. How do the numbers compare? Can you explain the difference? If the fan has variable settings, you can take readings at each setting (high, medium, low).

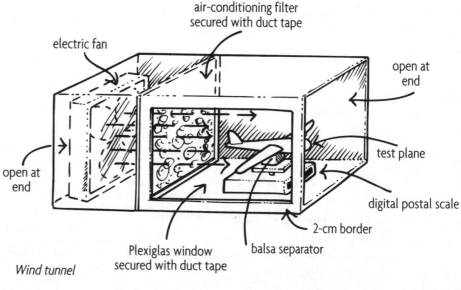

Wind tunnel

7. Test several different shaped objects and record their lift forces in a table. Analyze your results. Which shapes work best? You can also test the lift on paper airplanes and model airplanes, and relate your wind tunnel data to their actual performance when you fly them. Is there a correlation between the lift on a toy plane and the distance it flies?

References

Airplanes (What If . . . series) by Steve Parker (East Grinstead, Engl.: Copper Beech Books, 1995).

The Great International Paper Airplane Book (publication of the First International Paper Airplane Competition conducted by *Scientific American*) by Jerry Mander, George Dippel, and Howard Luck Gossage (New York: Galahad Books, 1998).

The Paper Airplane Book by Seymour Simon (Burnsville, Minn.: Econo-Clad Books, 1998).

Science Book of Air by Neil Ardley (San Diego: Harcourt, 1991).

"Caught in a Wind Tunnel" by Shawn Carlson: www.sciam.com/1197issue/1197amsci.html

Test-Flying Planes Underwater

The previous chapter described how to build a wind tunnel to study the aerodynamic properties of airfoils and planes. Here we study the hydrodynamic properties of planes underwater.

> *Hydro* means "water." **Hydrodynamics** is the study of the flow of water across surfaces, just as aerodynamics is the study of airflow.

The behavior of planes underwater is related to their flight ability. Although water is much denser than air, a plane that "flies" poorly underwater will probably have similar problems in the air.

> Common flight problems include sharp turns left or right, nosedives, and tailspins.

Materials

- plastic model plane
- water
- drill and bits (optional—*requires adult help*)
- about 0.5 kg wax (Candles will work.)
- Pyrex measuring cup and shallow pan (if using wax)
- stove or hot plate (if using wax—*requires adult help*)
- lard or petroleum jelly (optional)
- bathtub
- food coloring or nontoxic, water-soluble paint (optional)
- meterstick
- wax pencil or adhesive tape
- notebook and pencil
- thumbtacks and putty or soap
- file

Procedure

1. Prepare your plane for underwater flight. It is important that your plane does not float. You will have to fill it with water to give it ballast. You may need to ask an adult to make a couple of holes in the plane with a small drill bit. Sometimes it works better to fill the plane with wax. Have an adult melt the wax by heating it slowly in a Pyrex measuring cup nested in a shallow pan of water on a stove on low heat. When the wax is liquefied, ask an adult to pour some into your model plane. Allow the wax to cool. Alternatively, you can fill your plane with other substances, such as lard or petroleum jelly.

2. Fill your bathtub with warm water. (The reason for using warm water is simply to make it more comfortable for your hands, which will be underwater for a while.)

3. Do a test flight of your plane. Give it a gentle push underwater and study its behavior. Does it fly nicely, at an even speed, and nearly level? Or does it dive or turn?

4. Drop a few drops of food coloring or water-soluble paint from about 1 m

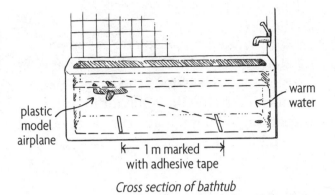

plastic model airplane

warm water

← 1 m marked →
with adhesive tape

Cross section of bathtub

above the tub. After the colors have passed through the water, fly the plane through the colored trail to see how the water moves. You should see small eddies, or whirling currents, as the plane passes through the water.

5. You can measure the glide ratio of your plane as follows:

   a. Make marks 1 m apart on the bottom of the tub, with either a wax pencil or strips of adhesive tape.

   b. Release the model from a point in the water above the first mark so that it glides to the bottom at the second mark. (This may take a few trials.)

   c. Measure the distance from the bottom of the tub to the place where you released the model plane.

   d. The **glide ratio** is easy to calculate—it is 100 divided by the altitude in centimeters at which the model was released.

6. You can make adjustments to your plane to help it compensate for poor flight.

   a. To manage balance, add a few thumbtacks stuck with putty or soap to the nose of the model. Plastic model planes (or paper airplanes for that matter) are sometimes too heavy in the rear.

   b. To straighten the flight path (keep the model from veering to the left or right), make adjustments to the vertical tail (or create one if it is missing), using thumbtacks and putty.

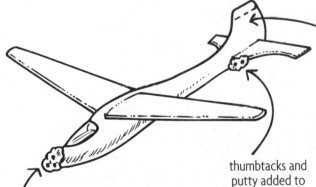

tail added to straighten flight path, or filed to prevent spiral dives

thumbtacks and putty added to straighten flight path

thumbtacks and putty added for balance

Adjustments to model plane

   c. Spiral dives indicate the plane is slightly tail heavy. Lighten the tail by filing away material, or weight the nose some more with tacks and putty.

7. Create thermals by letting the faucet run. A column of water moves up around the falling stream. When your model hits this gust of water, it will react exactly as a plane hitting a thermal in the air.

8. Create turbulence by pushing water toward the plane sharply with your submerged hand. This models how the plane would react to a gust of wind.

A **thermal** results from different air densities. Air that is cold relative to its surroundings is denser and sinks; hot air is less dense and rises, creating a thermal. **Turbulence** arises when the atmosphere has air pockets with differing temperatures. The eddying of these air masses pushes planes around, much to the discomfort of passengers.

---

9. Can you modify your plane to reduce the dangerous effects of thermals and turbulence? How does the mass of a plane determine its behavior in rough weather? What changes can you make to stabilize it?

References

Air and Space: The National Air and Space Museum Story of Flight by Andrew L. Chaikin and Sonian Smith (Boston: Bulfinch Press/Little, Brown, 2000).

100 Planes 100 Years: The First Century of Aviation by Fredric Winkowski and Frank D. Sullivan (New York: Smithmark, 1998).

The Cartesian Diver

When the density (mass divided by volume: $D = m/V$) of an object is greater than the density of the surrounding fluid or gas, the object sinks. When the density of the object is less, it rises. This is why ice floats in water and helium balloons in air, and why lead sinks in water and in air. Submarines control their own density by pumping seawater in and out of chambers. Divers wear weights to keep their density close to that of water; otherwise they would have to fight their tendency to float. A Cartesian diver is a simple device with a variable density that floats and sinks at your command.

Materials

- large widemouthed plastic jar with tight-fitting lid (A mayonnaise jar works well.)
- water
- eyedropper or pen cap
- clay or wire
- flat-sided plastic bottle
- soy sauce packet

Procedure

1. Fill a jar to the rim with water.

2. Put an eyedropper in the water and adjust it so that it barely floats. You can make these adjustments:

   a. If necessary, put some clay or wire around the tip to weight it so that it points downward.

   b. Adjust the amount of water inside the dropper. An air bubble is necessary in the top of the dropper.

   c. If the dropper sinks, make it lighter by reducing the water inside (increasing the air) or by removing some clay or wire from the tip. When the eyedropper is adjusted properly, if you push down on it, it should travel down for a bit, slowly come to a stop, and return to the surface.

3. Seal the lid on the jar. Now squeeze the sides of the jar. The diver should sink to the bottom until you release your grip.

As you squeeze the jar, you increase the pressure on the water and on the air bubble inside the dropper. This makes the bubble smaller. The reduced volume of the bubble makes the density of the diver greater than that of water, so it sinks. The density of water is 1 g/cc. This value is the basis of the metric system.

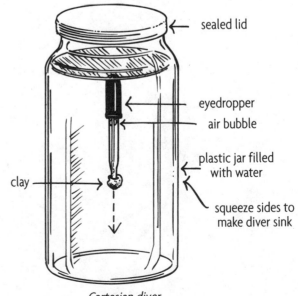

sealed lid

eyedropper

air bubble

plastic jar filled with water

clay

squeeze sides to make diver sink

Cartesian diver

4. Try these variations on the Cartesian diver:

a. If you do not have a dropper available, you can use a pen cap, which is open at one end.

b. With skill, you can get your diver to sink in a flat-sided glass bottle. Even glass bends under pressure.

c. Make a reverse Cartesian diver. Adjust the diver so it barely sinks to the bottom. Squeeze the jar a bit before sealing it. When you squeeze the jar gently at the bulge, the diver will rise from the reduced pressure of this configuration. This is because you are pushing the compressed sides outward, reducing the force they exert on the water inside. The air bubble in the Cartesian diver expands, and the loss of density makes the diver buoyant in the surrounding liquid.

> **Buoyancy** is an upward force exerted on an object by its surrounding medium (liquid or gas).

d. Make a "gourmet" diver. Use a sealed soy sauce packet as a diver. It usually has the right amount of air and liquid inside.

References

Diving into Darkness: A Submersible Explores the Sea by Rebecca L. Johnson (Minneapolis: Lerner, 1989).

Robert Fulton: From Submarine to Steamboat by Steven Kroll, Katherine Kirkpatrick, and Steve Kroll-Smith:(New York: Holiday House, 1999).

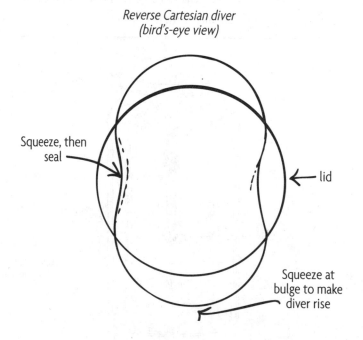

Reverse Cartesian diver (bird's-eye view)

Squeeze, then seal

lid

Squeeze at bulge to make diver rise

32 Color Addition

The three pure **primary colors** of light are red, green, and blue. When two primary colors of light mix, a **secondary color** results.

1. Red Light + Green Light ⟶ Yellow Light
2. Red Light + Blue Light ⟶ Magenta Light
3. Blue Light + Green Light ⟶ Cyan Light
4. White light is a mixture of all three primary colors:

    Blue Light + Green Light + Red Light ⟶ White Light

If you're scratching your head and saying, "But red and green paint make brown!" it's because paint colors combine by color subtraction, not color addition. The pigments in paint **filter** (block out) reflected light. In pigments the primary colors are red, yellow, and blue. **Color addition** is the process of blending differently colored lights together, such as shining different colored theater lights onto a stage. The more colored lights you add to the blend, the brighter and whiter the results. **Color subtraction** is the process of successively filtering out colors. If you look through several pairs of different colored sunglasses, you can observe color subtraction. Similarly, the more colors of paint or dye you mix, the more you subtract and the darker and blacker the results.

Materials

- 3 focused light sources (slide projectors or theater lights)
- white screen
- tape
- colored gels or filters—red, blue, and green

Why is the sky blue? The atmosphere **refracts** (bends and changes the velocity of) light into different colors as a prism does. Blue is refracted the most, so it bends back to our eyes. For the same reason, water in the ocean **reflects** light rays, bouncing them off the surface, so the ocean often appears blue. (For more on refraction and reflecting, see the next chapter.)

- prism
- scissors
- cardboard
- drawing compass
- metric ruler
- cordless drill with sanding disk or buffing wheel bit (*requires adult help*)
- glue
- safety goggles
- white paper
- markers or paint and paintbrush

Procedure

To Demonstrate Color Addition with Gels

1. Aim your three light sources at a white screen in a dark room. They should overlap, but not completely (see figure).

2. Tape gels or filters in front of each light to make the three primary colors of light (red, blue, green) fall on the screen.

3. The three secondary colors of light (cyan, yellow, and magenta) will appear where two primary colors overlap. At the intersection of all three colors, you will see white. (You may have to experiment with different shades of gels, or double up some colors, to get ideal results.)

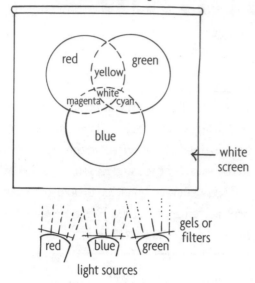

Color addition with gels

white screen

gels or filters

red   blue   green

light sources

Isaac Newton split a narrow beam of white light into the colors of the spectrum—red, orange, yellow, green, blue, indigo, violet—using a prism in a dark room. You can, too.

To Demonstrate Color Addition with a Color Wheel

1. Cut out a circular cardboard disk, 15 to 20 cm in diameter. Devise a method of mounting the disk on a drill so that the disk spins. One way to do this is to have an adult center the disk on a sanding disk or buffing wheel bit and fasten it securely with glue. Use caution when you operate the drill—wear goggles and don't touch the spinning disk.

2. Cut out a white paper disk of the same size, and use markers or paint to color it red, green, and blue in pie slices. Glue it to the cardboard wheel.

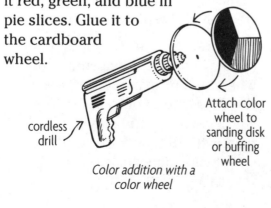

cordless drill

Attach color wheel to sanding disk or buffing wheel

Color addition with a color wheel

3. Spin the color wheel as fast as you can and observe the resulting color.

Since your colors are not likely to be pure and the same intensity, you will probably have to vary the size of the pie slices to get white—which may be closer to cream in color. In both activities, you can make a table of primary, secondary, and more complex (tertiary) colors as shown. (Fill in the blanks based on your experimentation.)

COLOR ADDITION OF LIGHT

Red	Green	Blue	Result
100%	100%	0%	yellow
100%	0%	——	magenta
0%	100%	100%	————
100%	100%	100%	————
0%	——	——	black
100%	50%	50%	peach
——	——	——	cyan

References

The Magic Wand and Other Bright Experiments on Light and Color (Exploratorium Science Snackbook series) by Paul Doherty (New York: John Wiley & Sons, 1991).

The Optics Book: Fun Experiments with Light, Vision, and Color by Sharon Levine and Leslie Johnstone (New York: Sterling, 1998).

Make a Splash with Color: www.TheTech.org/exhibits_events/online/color/intro/

33 Studying Wave Properties in a Ripple Tank

Waves are a form of energy derived from the periodic motion of a solid, liquid, or gas. You are probably most familiar with them in water; however, waves can travel through other substances, such as gases and solids. The substance a wave travels through is called the **medium.** Sound is produced by waves in air. Waves move in straight lines and at constant velocities through uniform mediums. Waves can even travel through a vacuum, in the form of electromagnetic radiation such as light and radio waves.

Sound waves travel approximately 340 m per second through air. Light waves travel nearly a million times faster, at 300 million m per second.

All waves exhibit various properties that you can demonstrate: reflection, refraction, diffraction, and interference. (For more on interference, see chapter 34, "Wave Interference.")

Materials

- large, shallow, clear glass pan
- clear glass- or plastic-topped coffee table (or table-size piece of Plexiglas and 2 sawhorses)
- lamp with 100-watt clear incandescent bulb or other bright, concentrated light source
- room with a white ceiling
- water
- metric ruler
- pen or pencil
- stopwatch
- notebook
- wire cutters
- 1-m section of rubber tubing (An old garden hose works well.)
- wire coat hanger or other firm wire
- small, rectangular clear plate (Suggested dimensions are 5 by 5 by 0.5 cm. You can ask a hardware store to cut the square from acrylic or glass and have them dull the edges with sandpaper so they do not cut you.)

Procedure

To Set Up the Ripple Tank

1. Use a shallow glass pan, the bigger the better. Place it on a clear coffee table through which you can see the floor. Alternatively, you can support the pan on a table-size piece of Plexiglas placed across a pair of sawhorses. It is important that the center is unobstructed. Place a bright light under the pan, aimed upward at the ceiling. It is best to choose a room with a plain white ceiling.

2. Check the pan for stability. Add a small quantity of water, to a depth of 1 to 2 cm.

3. Turn off the room lights. Take a capped pen or a pencil and gently tap the water once, briefly dipping the tip under the surface. Look at the waves in

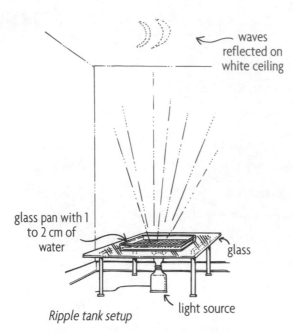

waves
reflected on
white ceiling ←

glass pan with 1
to 2 cm of
water

glass

light source

Ripple tank setup

the pan and their reflection on the ceiling. Notice how the waves move outward from the disturbance, travel through the water, and bounce off the sides.

> Eventually the wave energy **dissipates** (disperses or moves away from the source), leaving the surface of the water calm again.

Tap the surface multiple times to create a repeated source of waves for several seconds. Practice both techniques.

> You can calculate the velocity of the wave with a stopwatch. Velocity equals distance divided by time. Divide the distance it takes a wave to cross the pan by the time, and you'll have the wave's velocity.

To Demonstrate Reflection

1. Using wire cutters, cut a short 10-to-15-cm length of tube. Cut a piece of firm coat hanger wire to the same length. Pass the wire into the tube. You should be able to bend or straighten the tube. Adjust the tube so that it is straight,

then lay it in the center of the ripple tank to create a barrier. The top half of the barrier should be above the surface of the water. Adjust the water level if necessary.

2. Create a wave disturbance 10 cm away from one side of the barrier. Notice how the waves bounce off the barrier at an angle.

> You have just demonstrated **Snell's law:** The **angle of incidence** (angle at which light strikes a surface) is equal to the **angle of reflection** (angle at which light reflects off a surface). This is written $\angle i = \angle r$.

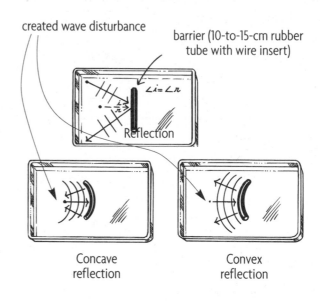

created wave disturbance

barrier (10-to-15-cm rubber tube with wire insert)

$\angle i = \angle r$

Reflection

Concave reflection

Convex reflection

3. Bend the barrier into a curve, then put it back in the water. Make a wave disturbance in the middle of the concave side. (A **concave** curve bends inward— think "cave." A **convex** curve bends outward.) Notice how the waves bounce back toward a central area or **focal point.** The waves are said to **converge**.

> If you bend the barrier into a parabola, all the waves will converge on a focal point (For information on parabolas, see chapter 4, "Demonstrating Orbits.")

Now make a disturbance on the convex side. The waves **diverge** outward from the focal point.

To Demonstrate Refraction

1. Remove the barrier and place a rectangular plate in the pan. If you use glass less than 0.5 cm thick, you may need to stack two or three plates. Press the plate(s) down firmly in the center of the pan.

2. Create a wave disturbance on one side of the pan. Notice that as the waves pass over the plate, they change speed relative to those passing by the sides. When waves enter a new medium (here, shallower water is the new medium), they change speed. This is called **refraction.**

> Light waves refract when they go from air to water, or air to glass. Otherwise, how could we see those clear substances at all?

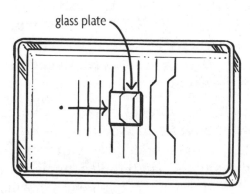

Refraction

To Demonstrate Diffraction

1. Make another barrier out of tubing as you did in step 1 of the reflection experiment. Place the two barriers in the middle of the pan so that they are end to end separated by a small gap.

2. Send a wave toward the gap. Notice how the waves emerge on the other side out of the gap. Obstacles and small openings **diffract** (change the direction and intensity of) waves.

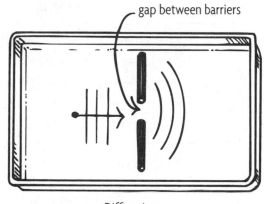

Diffraction

References

Making Waves: Finding Out about Rhythmic Motion (Boston Children's Museum Activity Book) by Bernie Zubrowski (New York: Morrow/Avon, 1994).

Waves: The Electromagnetic Universe by Gloria Skurzynski (Washington, D.C.: National Geographic Society, 1996).

Making Waves: www.li.net/~stmarya/stm/home.htm

"Tsunami!" by Frank I. Gonzalez: www.sciam.com/1999/0599issue/0599gonzalez.html

Physics 34 Wave Interference

Interference is a property of light that can be observed when different sets of light waves mix together. Examples of interference include the rainbows you see in soap bubbles, the colorful spectrum of opals, and the shimmering colors of some bird feathers. In some regions of interference patterns, the waves of light are in phase, with matching peaks and troughs, creating bright zones. In other regions, they are out of phase, with opposing

> Interference results from overlapping waves. When two wave **peaks** (high points) meet, they combine into a larger wave. When a wave peak and a wave **trough** (low point) meet, the waves cancel each other out. The positions of peaks and troughs are called **phases.**

peaks and troughs, creating dim zones. There are a variety of ways to demonstrate interference, both as bright and dim regions, and as different colors representing the different wavelengths of light.

Materials

- shallow baking pan
- water
- chopsticks or 2 pens and a rubberband, or a Y-shaped object
- some or all of the following: bubble solution, opal jewelry, feathers, two 20-cm-square pieces of cut window glass with edges finished. (A hardware store can cut glass to order. Ask them to sand the edges for you to make it safe to handle.)
- various light sources (bulbs, laser pointer, lab laser, ordinary flashlight, flashlight with lens)

- convex lens
- sheet of paper or dollar bill
- 2 stands with clamps
- white screen or wall
- discarded projector slides
- scissors
- transparent tape
- black construction paper
- black spray paint
- thumbtacks
- one-hole paper punch
- leather punch
- ball bearing

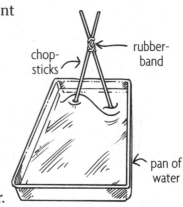

Procedure

1. Fill a shallow pan with water. Fasten two chopsticks together with a rubber band to make a two-pronged disturbance source. Tap the water with the chopsticks (or tap two fingers, two pens, or a Y-shaped object) and observe the patterns that result when waves from the two disturbances intersect. Where waves combine, you get larger waves (**constructive interference**). Where they cancel each other out, you get calm spots (**destructive interference**).

2. Examine a variety of materials where **optical interference** causes patterns of light and dark, or colored patterns. You can examine soap bubbles, opals, and bird feathers. If you live near a marina, you can observe the water where a drop or two of oil has spilled from the

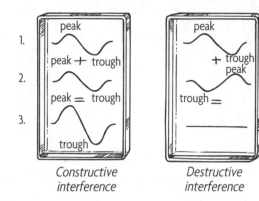

Constructive
interference

Destructive
interference

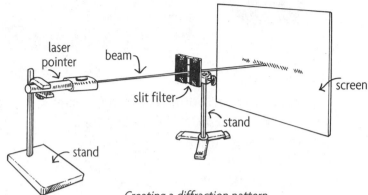

Creating a diffraction pattern

boats—colored rainbows are emitted from the expanding layer of oil as it spreads across the surface. You can create optical interference patterns by sandwiching two thin, smooth plates of glass together. Aim a light source at them, and press them together. Shimmering rings of light and dark, with colored hues, become visible.

Vary the effect by creating a small gap between the plates at one edge, using a piece of paper or a dollar bill.

> Alternatively, substitute a convex lens from an old pair of glasses or broken camera for one of the pieces of glass, and examine what happens when you press the lens against the glass.

3. Use two stands with clamps to set up a laser pointer so that its beam passes through a slit filter onto a white screen or wall. (You can make a slit filter with an old photographic slide. Cut out the plastic image, and tape two black paper rectangles in its place, close together, leaving a uniform slit running vertically down the middle.) In one of the great mysteries of light, the beam passing through the filter magically creates regions of light and dark called **a diffraction pattern.** Replace the slit

filter with other types of filters: slits of different widths and shapes; holes of different sizes; a lens in front of a ball bearing.

> To fashion filters with different holes, take some old, unneeded slides and darken them with black spray paint. Then punch different size holes in them, using thumbtacks, a paper punch, and a leather punch.

4. You can change certain variables in your setup to create a more formal experiment. Vary the light source to compare the differences between a laser pointer, a lab laser, an ordinary flashlight, a flashlight with a lens, and bulbs of different types. Or study the diffraction pattern on the screen as a function of distance between the laser and the filter, and/or the filter and the screen.

References

Awesome Experiments in Light and Sound by Michael Anthony Dispezio (New York: Sterling, 2000).

Making Waves: Finding Out about Rhythmic Motion (Boston Children's Museum Activity Book) by Bernie Zubrowski (New York: Morrow/Avon, 1994).

35 Studying Liquid Vortices

A **vortex,** or whirlpool, is a liquid or gas flowing about an axis. Vortices appear in nature on large and small scales. The small swirl of water in a draining sink is a vortex. The devastating winds of tornadoes and hurricanes are also vortices. You can easily build an apparatus to study liquid vortices with scientific precision.

Materials

- 2-L soda bottle with extra caps
- scissors
- one-hole paper punch
- metric ruler
- drill and bits (*requires adult help*)
- ring stand and 2 clamps (One ring clamp should be larger in diameter than the bottle, the other smaller.)
- three 15-cm pieces of uninsulated wire
- food coloring
- notebook and pencil
- small cork
- 30-cm string
- timer
- tubing (Latex and Tygon tubing work well. The tube should be large enough to fit over the faucet. A hardware store can sell you a special adapter that will screw into the faucet. You may find you get better results if your tube runs from the faucet to a second tube of narrower diameter.)

Procedure

To Assemble the Apparatus

1. Cut off the bottom of a soda bottle with scissors. Punch three holes about 4 cm apart around the bottom edge of the bottle, using a paper punch.

2. Ask an adult to drill a hole in the center of the cap. You should try different size holes to see which is best for making vortices. If you have extra caps, use a range of bits from 1 to 2.5 cm to make a different size hole in each cap. If you have only one cap, start with the smallest bit and make the hole larger with each trial.

3. Screw the cap on the bottle, then mount the bottle upside down in the sink. You can do this by placing the mouth of the bottle through a small ring clamp that supports it, and encircling the bottle at the middle with a larger clamp.

4. Connect one end of a tube to the faucet. Mount the other end inside the bottom edge of the bottle. Several centimeters of the end of the tube should be horizontal, following the inside curve of the bottle. Pass a piece of wire through each punched hole and twist the ends to fasten the tube in place.

5. Turn on the water, starting with a gentle flow and increasing slowly.

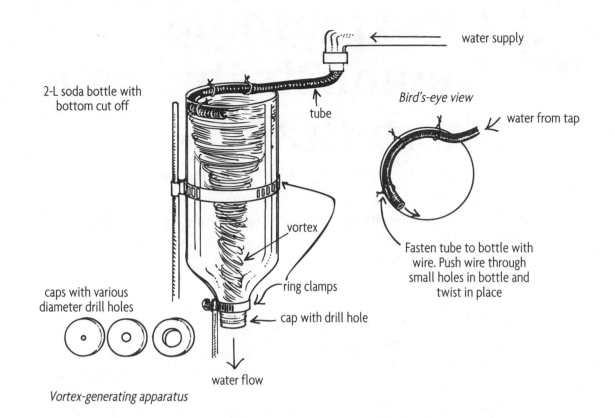

2-L soda bottle with bottom cut off

water supply

tube

Bird's-eye view

water from tap

vortex

Fasten tube to bottle with wire. Push wire through small holes in bottle and twist in place

caps with various diameter drill holes

ring clamps

cap with drill hole

water flow

Vortex-generating apparatus

To Explore the Vortex Effect

1. At what water elevation in the bottle do vortices begin to form?

> Vortices can be a problem. Vortices in the wake of ships and aircraft waste fuel because they use up energy. Vortices become a serious menace during forest fires because they are capable of picking up large flaming timbers and dropping them elsewhere to start new fires.

2. What are the dimensions of a vortex?

3. Drop food coloring slowly into the water and sketch the path of the water. What can you determine about how vortices form?

4. What diameter hole works best for producing vortices?

5. Hang a small cork from a string in the vortex to measure the number of revolutions per minute of the water. Determine this value (a) at the mouth of the vortex and (b) at different depths in the vortex.

> Vortices occur in air and water because these substances exhibit the properties of friction and adhesion—they rub together and stick to themselves to some degree. Release a drop of detergent into a vortex and watch it disappear as the surface tension of the water is chemically destroyed. (Adhesion and surface tension are explained in the next chapter.)

References

Hurricanes and Tornadoes (When Disaster Strikes series) by Keith Greenberg (Chicago: Twenty-First Century Books, 1995).

Hurricanes and Tornadoes by Neil Morris (Hauppauge, N.Y.: Barron's, 1999).

Physics 36 Gravitational Field Demonstrated in a Soap Bubble

To the scientist, soap bubbles are more than a visual delight. They demonstrate and model many principles of chemistry and physics: adhesion, cohesion, surface tension, and elasticity.

> **Cohesion** is the attraction between molecules of the same substance, such as soap solution to itself.
> **Adhesion** is the attraction between molecules of different substances, such as soap to a countertop. The soap bubble exhibits **surface tension** (contraction) as the membrane of soap is stretched around a bubble of slightly pressurized air. The bubble is **elastic:** it stretches and contracts.

You can also use soap bubbles to model physics phenomena, in this case, gravitational fields. (Gravity is a weak mutual force of attraction between all matter.)

Materials

- mixing bowl
- metric measuring cup and spoons
- water
- dishwashing liquid
- glycerin (available at drugstores)
- stirring rod or spoon
- wineglass
- wire (Coat hanger wire is fine.)
- wire cutters
- metric ruler
- quick-set waterproof epoxy
- baking pan
- ring stand and clamps
- rubber tubing to hold dropper
- dropper pipette or eyedropper
- food coloring
- toothbrush

Procedure

1. In a mixing bowl, mix up a batch of soap bubbles. The best solutions are not pure soap, but rather a specific solution of different ingredients. Start with a ratio of 500 mL of cold tap water to 50 mL of dishwashing liquid and 3 mL of glycerin. Different brands of detergent give different results, so switch brands if you are not satisfied with your bubbles. Mix the ingredients well by gently stirring.

2. Devise your bubble-generating apparatus. Instead of being blown, the bubbles will hang from a ring-shaped frame.

> To do a quick demonstration of the bubble ring, simply invert a wineglass, dip the rim in your soap solution, and lift the glass up.

a. Fashion the bubble ring from a 35-cm piece of wire. Join the ends of the ring together with quick-set waterproof epoxy and allow the epoxy to harden.

b. Make a U-shaped wire bar and attach it to opposite sides of the ring, with two wire struts, each 8 cm long, rising up as shown. The struts will allow you to handle the ring. Join the pieces of wire with epoxy.

c. Fill a baking pan with bubble solution.

d. Arrange a ring stand to clamp the bubble ring above the pan so that your hands are free.

e. Remove the bulb of a dropper, and attach 1 m of rubber tubing to the exposed base of the dropper. The tube should fit snugly over the base.

3. Generate bubbles and simulate planetary orbits, gravitation, and formation.

a. Gently dip the ring into the pan, allowing it to get completely covered in bubble solution.

b. Slowly lift the ring out so that a circular bubble film forms in the ring. Fasten the struts to the stand. Notice that the film hangs from its own weight.

> You may notice colorful interference patterns in the soap film during the first few minutes of its life. (See chapter 34 "Wave Interference.")

c. Dip the dropper in the soap solution to get a drop in the tip. It may help to put your finger over the open end of the tube after submersing the dropper tip.

d. Release the drop in the bubble film. Aim it, as best you can, tangential to the circumference of the circle. The drop should spiral inward toward the center.

e. Watch the drops move in an orbit similar to that of planets about the Sun. You may vary the initial speed

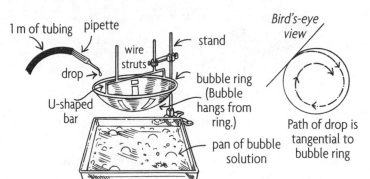

Bubble-generating apparatus

> A line that is **tangential** to a circle touches it at one point, as shown.

of the drop by giving a gentle blow from the open end of the tube. Try to release two or more drops in the same run. They will travel and interact like multiple planets in a solar system; or like moons about a planet.

f. To simulate the formation of a star or planet, use a toothbrush to spray fine droplets of solution onto a fresh bubble film and let the droplets coalesce into one drop. The spray represents an interstellar gas cloud, and the drop a star.

> When two drops collide, the more massive one usually absorbs the smaller one, like a black hole colliding with a star. By coloring one drop with food coloring and waiting until both drops merge, you can see that they will spin violently about an axis.

References

Black Holes and Neutron Stars:
antwrp.gsfc.nasa.gov/htmltest/rjn_bht.html

Family Fun magazine on soap bubbles:
www.family.go.com/features/family_1997_07/
famf/famf77bubbles/

Building a Periscope

All you need to make a **periscope** is two mirrors and something on which to mount them. Then you can see around and over barriers, spy above walls, and study animals without disturbing them. Periscopes are used in submarines to see above the water; but with special materials and some effort you can build a periscope to see down into the water. Adding lenses to your periscope in the right combination can improve the viewing experience.

Be sure to read this activity in its entirety before you begin (as you should with all activities). There are several variations on design, and the one you choose will determine your approach and materials.

Materials

- 60-by-90-by-0.3-cm sheet of Plexiglas or plywood (available at hardware stores)
- meterstick
- black spray paint
- silicone aquarium or bathroom sealant (optional)
- 2 small mirrors

> For mirrors, you can use dental mirrors. Have an adult use a jeweler's saw to saw off each handle near the mirror, leaving the mirror in the plastic mount.

- 2 weak convex lenses (from an old pair of eyeglasses or available from science suppliers, such as Edmund Scientific—optional)
- epoxy (if using lenses)

For Plexiglas Periscope

- Plexiglas cutter (a scorer that cuts a small groove to enable you to break the Plexiglas cleanly—*requires adult help*)
- plastic glue
- duct tape and scissors

For Plywood Periscope

- table saw (*requires adult help*)
- waterproof paint (optional)
- finishing nails and hammer
- Plexiglas to cover openings (optional)

Procedure

1. Build the body of your periscope from Plexiglas or plywood.

   a. Design and build a long four-sided chamber with openings at opposite sides of each end, as shown. The dimensions of the side walls are up to you—a good size to start with is 70 by 4 cm. Your device will operate best if you paint the inside walls black before assembling.

   b. If using Plexiglas, have an adult cut the walls of the periscope and join them with plastic glue. Allow the glue to dry.

   c. If using plywood, have an adult use a table saw to cut out the walls.

   d. If you intend to use your periscope in the water, join all edges with aquarium sealant. You will want to treat the plywood with an undercoat of a couple coats of waterproof paint after applying the sealant.

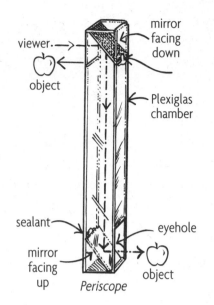

Periscope

e. In some cases, it may be useful to reinforce your periscope with thin strips of duct tape (for Plexiglas) or small finishing nails (for plywood).

2. Lay your periscope flat on a table and position the mirrors parallel to each other, at each opening, with the reflective surfaces facing each other. Adjust them so that when you look in one opening (the eyehole), you can see distant objects through the other opening (the viewer). When the mirrors are lined up properly (calibrated), glue them to the sides with aquarium sealant.

> You can widen the field of view in your periscope by adding a weak convex lens next to each mirror, positioned parallel to each other and to the ends of the periscope. Use epoxy to affix the lenses. Things will look smaller than they do in real life, but you will be able to see more.

3. When your periscope is dry, practice viewing through it. Look over a wall, under a table, around a corner, and down a hole.

To Make an Underwater Periscope

If you have made your periscope with waterproof walls, you may want to take the mirror near the eyehole out so you can look straight down into the periscope. This will be more comfortable when you are leaning over a dock. The only remaining openings should be at the eyehole and the viewer, where the light travels in and out. Cover the openings with slightly larger pieces of Plexiglas, and glue them in place with sealant. Allow the pieces to dry overnight, and inspect carefully for leaks. If you have a good seal, you can dip the lower end into a pond and start using your viewing instrument to study underwater ecology.

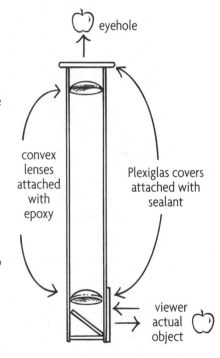

Underwater and lens modifications

References

Experiments with Light and Mirrors (Getting Started in Science series) by Robert Gardner (Berkeley Heights, N.J.: Enslow, 1995).

Making Light Work: The Science of Optics (Xperiment! series) by David Darling (Parsippany, N.J.: Silver Burdette, 1991).

The Optics Book: Fun Experiments with Light, Vision and Color by Sharon Levine and Leslie Johnstone (New York: Sterling, 1998).

Kite Flying

Kites are readily available for purchase in many stores. However, the experience of flying a kite is much more rewarding when you have constructed the kite yourself. By experimenting with the design, and trying to obtain the maximum possible altitude, you can learn about aerodynamics and engineering. (For more on aerodynamics, see chapter 29, "Experiments in a Wind Tunnel.")

Kites have different functions. Fighting kites are used to attack each other in contests. Acrobatic kites can dive, loop, and perform figure eights. Some kites are designed to appeal to the eye and ear. These kites range in form from simple diamond shapes to figures resembling birds, animals, and mythological creatures, including dragons up to 30 m long. The kites are usually multicolored and may carry bamboo pipes and other instruments that emit musical sounds.

Materials

- thin spruce sticks 0.5 cm thick, or ¼-in. dowel stock
- fine-tooth wood saw (*requires adult help*)
- meterstick
- knife (*requires adult help*)
- glue
- 160 m of thin nylon string, available at hardware stores (*not* wire!)
- scissors
- kite cloth (newspaper, closely woven silk, or Mylar)
- kite string spool
- strip of cloth for tail

- 4 paper cups or pint-sized ice cream cartons (if not using cloth)
- bamboo (optional)
- small camera or weather-sensing instruments (optional)

Procedure

1. Construct a simple diamond-shaped kite—a pair of crossed sticks covered with paper.

   a. Have an adult use a fine-tooth wood saw to cut the sticks. Make the spline, or vertical stick, 100 cm long, and the spar, or horizontal stick, 67 cm long. Have adult use a knife to make a 2-mm notch at both ends of each stick.

   b. Position the sticks so that the middle of the spar crosses the middle of the spline 33 cm from the top of the spline. Fasten the sticks together where they cross, using a drop of glue and a binding of string.

   c. When the glue dries, run a string around the sticks through the notches.

   d. Cut a piece of kite cloth as shown, fold the edges over the string, and secure it with glue.

   e. Fit the kite with a **bridle,** a short span of string tied to the top and bottom ends of the spline on the cloth-covered side of the kite, and a span tied to each end of the spar. (The length of each span is determined by the dimensions and flexibility of the kite.) Adjust the bridle length so that the strings become taut when pulled 30 cm from the

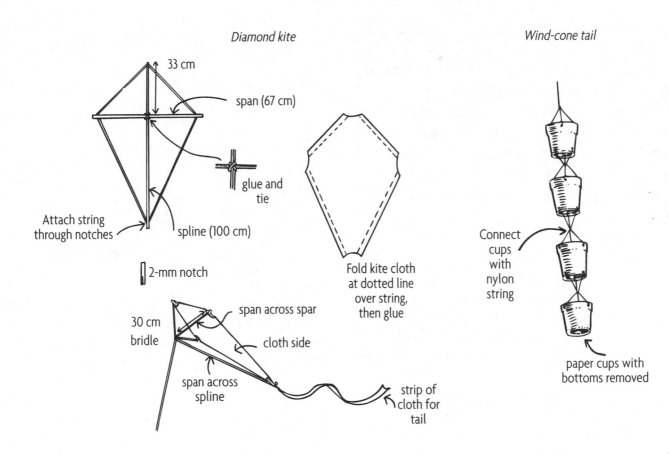

Diamond kite

33 cm

span (67 cm)

glue and tie

Attach string through notches

spline (100 cm)

2-mm notch

30 cm bridle

span across spar

cloth side

span across spline

Fold kite cloth at dotted line over string, then glue

strip of cloth for tail

Wind-cone tail

Connect cups with nylon string

paper cups with bottoms removed

cloth at a point directly above where the sticks cross.

f. Wind 150 m of string on a spool. This is your flying string. Temporarily tie the free end of the flying string to the bridle at the point determined in step 1e. The point at which the flying

Kites, like the mainsail of a sailboat, perform best at angles of attack ranging from about 20 to 25 degrees, greater than the angle at which an airplane wing meets the wind because of the pronounced curvature of the paper. The exact angle of attack at which a kite performs best depends on the strength of the wind and must be determined experimentally. The adjustment is accomplished by shifting the flying string toward the top of the kite.

string is attached to the bridle determines the angle at which the air strikes the kite: the angle of attack.

g. Diamond kites are unstable until you fit them with a tail to hold them upright. A tail can simply be a strip of cloth tied to the base of the spline. Alternatively you can provide the kite with a tail that consists of a series of wind cones (see figure). The cones can be made by removing the bottoms from four paper containers, such as paper cups or ice cream cartons. Connect the cups with nylon string.

2. Fly your kite in a safe place, such as an open field at least 1 km from any power lines or airports. Never fly a kite when the string is wet or the weather is bad.

The stabilizing force is provided partly by the weight of the tail, partly by friction between the tail and the moving air, and partly by turbulence generated in the airstream by the tail. The last two forces are known as **drag.** The amount of stability required increases with the speed of the wind. A kite that flies nicely with a short tail during a light breeze will spin out of control in a stiff wind. Yet a kite with a long tail that flies well in a stiff wind may not fly in a light breeze.

a. To launch your kite, grasp the spool of flying string in one hand and the bottom of the kite in the other.

> A circular kite can be made by bending bamboo into a hoop.

b. Incline the kite at an angle of about 25 degrees into the wind, with the cloth side facing the wind, and let it go.

c. As the kite rises, play out the flying string at a rate that allows the kite to continue its ascent.

3. Experiment with different design changes. You can vary the following:

a. The length of the spline and the spar.

b. The shape of the kite. For example, three sticks of equal length can be crossed to make a hexagonal kite.

c. The construction materials.

d. The length and weight of the tail.

e. The number of kites. You can send up a train of two or more kites.

f. The payload (cargo). For example, you can send up a small camera or weather-sensing instruments.

On May 5, 1910, the uppermost unit in a train of 10 Weather Bureau kites carried a payload of meteorological instruments to an altitude of 8,000 m. The kite exerted a pull of nearly 0.25 ton on the 14.5-km flying string of piano wire.

References

The Great Kite Book by Norman Schmidt (New York: Sterling, 1998).

Making Kites (Step-by-Step) by David Michael and David Jefferis (Stanwood, Wa.: Kingfisher, 1993).

A Rubber Band Heat Engine

Most materials expand when heated. Bridges and sidewalks are constructed with gaps between solid sections so that the sections have room to expand in the summer heat. In cold weather, the sections contract and the gaps get larger. Train wheels are heated before being placed on their axles so that when they cool off, they contract and hang on tightly. A metal ball that just barely passes through a ring will get stuck if heated, but passes easily after being plunged into ice water.

Not so with rubber bands under tension. Heat a stretched rubber band, and it will contract; cool it off, and it will expand. Its strange behavior has to do with the chainlike structure of the rubber molecules.

> Picture rubber under tension as a bundle of stretched chains, with heat shaking the chains. The harder the chains are shaken, the more they pull on their ends, thus contracting.

You can use the unusual thermal properties of rubber bands to create a heat-responsive apparatus. It won't power a locomotive, but you'll get an idea of how a **heat engine** (a machine that transforms heat into mechanical energy) could work on a larger scale.

Materials
- safety goggles (for use when heating and handling rubber bands)
- a variety of rubber bands
- 2 ring stands (or fashion stands out of materials of your own, such as camera tripods or scrap wood)
- metric ruler
- 2 to 4 clamps and a pulley (You can find all kinds of clamps and pulleys in a home improvement or hardware store.)
- scissors
- 1 to 3 hooked lab weights
- correction fluid
- ice
- timer
- heat lamp or blow-dryer
- wire (optional)

Procedure

> Put on your safety goggles and hold a rubber band in front of you. Before stretching it, touch it to your lip to feel the temperature. Now stretch it long and tight, quickly, and bring it back to your lip, keeping it stretched. Feel the warmth? You performed work on the rubber band, and the energy you gave it became converted to heat. After waiting a few seconds for the rubber band (still stretched), to return to room temperature, release the tension quickly and let it contract, bringing it once more to your lip. It should feel cold now, as it absorbs heat.

1. Set up two stands adjacent to each other, approximately 20 cm apart. You can adjust this distance as needed to accommodate your rubber band.

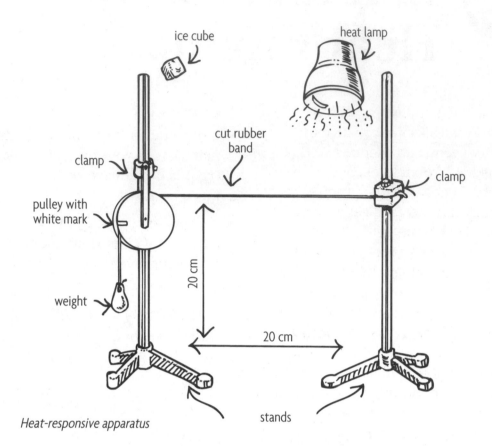

ice cube

heat lamp

cut rubber band

clamp

clamp

pulley with white mark

20 cm

weight

20 cm

Heat-responsive apparatus

stands

2. Clamp a pulley to one stand, about 20 cm above the base, so that the plane of the pulley is vertically oriented.

3. Cut the rubber band and clamp one end to the other stand at the same height as the pulley. Pass the other end over the pulley. (If your stands move, you may need to place weights on them or clamp them to a table.)

4. Hang a weight on the free end of the rubber band so that the rubber band stretches over the pulley and the weight hangs freely. Mark a spot on the pulley with a stripe of correction fluid, like a radio dial. Note the location of the mark.

5. Gently rub an ice cube along the rubber band, back and forth, for 1 minute.

What happens to the dial on the pulley?

6. Aim the heat lamp at the rubber band. Now what happens?

7. As an extension, you can redesign your apparatus for maximum sensitivity and movement. Vary the length and type of rubber bands. Experiment with bundles of rubber bands, or other materials, such as wire. When you use wire, how will the motion of the pulley differ from when you use rubber?

References

How Machines Work by Christopher Rawson (Tulsa, Okla.: EDC Publishing, 1983).

Science Magic with Machines (Science Magic series) by Chris Oxlade (Hauppauge, N.Y.: Barron's Juveniles, 1995).

Electric Circuits

With some materials scrounged from the basement or attic and a few dollars' investment, you can model typical electric circuits and make new designs of your own. If you make any good inventions, patent them and sell your ideas!

> Thomas Edison (1847–1931) searched for years to find the best materials and methods for manufacturing lightbulbs. One of the best designs, tungsten filaments in a vacuum or in a noble gas, is still used today.

Materials

- wire strippers
- insulated wire (copper phone line, old lamp cord, or speaker wire)
- metric ruler
- power supply (6-volt lantern battery, or power supply from an old external computer modem or answering machine)
- electronic components with screw terminals (minilight fixtures and doorbells)
- several wire nuts
- electric tape
- other assorted components: low-voltage (3-to-12-volt) lightbulbs, single- and double-throw knife switches (single-pole), doorbell button, buzzers, LEDs, small electric motors, photosensitive resistors (available at hardware stores or RadioShack)

- test equipment: ampmeter and voltmeter, or multitester (available at RadioShack)

Procedure

To Assemble the Components

1. Use wire strippers to remove the insulation and expose the bare wire. If your wire is a bundle of smaller wires, remove the outer insulation first. Sometimes you can make a small cut and pull an inner wire along the incision, tearing the insulation open. The insulation falls away, exposing the inner wires. Then cut the single strands to workable lengths—20 cm is a good length—and strip 1 to 2 cm of insulation off each end.

2. Read the power supply specifications and see what it delivers. The input should be 120 volts (V) AC, plugging into your wall. The output should be 5 to 15V DC, 100 to 500 milliamps (mA) of

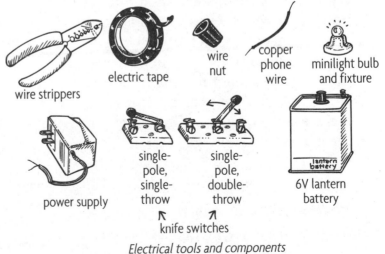

wire strippers • electric tape • wire nut • copper phone wire • minilight bulb and fixture

power supply • single-pole, single-throw / single-pole, double-throw — knife switches • 6V lantern battery

Electrical tools and components

current. An **amp** (ampere) is a unit of electric current, and a **volt** is a unit of electrical potential difference and electromotive force. If you think of an electric current as water flowing in a hose, the amount of water is the amperage, and the speed of the water is the voltage. To find out why amperage kills, and voltage doesn't, see the next chapter.

3. Components that have screw terminals, such as minilight fixtures or doorbells are useful. You connect a wire to other components and wires by wrapping it around the terminal screw and tightening it, by twisting the two wires together. The exposed connections can be covered by twisting them on a wire nut or wrapping them with electric tape.

4. Use low-voltage bulbs (3 to 12V) matched as closely to your power supply as possible. It's easier to work with bulbs if you have fixtures you screw them into, with screw terminals. Get some knife switches or doorbell buttons. Knife switches come in different types—a couple of single- and double-throw switches will suffice. You can mix and match other components, such as buzzers, light-emitting diodes, (LEDs), motors, and photosensitive resistors. Amp- and voltmeters are useful test equipment to determine the current and voltage present in the circuit.

To Build and Test Circuits

1. Get to know the symbols here as you build each circuit. Once you learn how

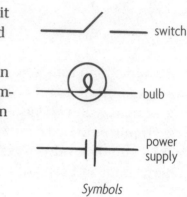

Symbols

to read circuit diagrams and build from them, you can use these symbols to design new circuits before handling the equipment.

a. Circuit 1 is a simple circuit with a power supply, two wires, and a bulb. Each terminal of the bulb leads to one terminal of the power supply. The bulb goes on when the circuit is completed. To turn the bulb off, disconnect one wire from the power supply.

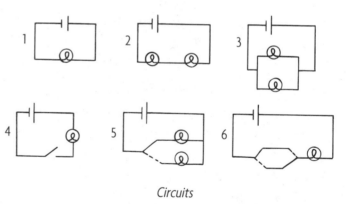

Circuits

b. Circuit 2 has two bulbs in a series circuit. Each bulb will be about half as bright as the bulb in circuit 1 because the voltage is split between the two bulbs. The electric current passes successively through each component.

Use a voltmeter and ampmeter (or a multitester, both meters in the same device) to analyze **series** and **parallel circuits.**

c. Circuit 3 has two bulbs in a parallel circuit. Both bulbs receive the full voltage and should be as bright as the bulb in circuit 1. The electric current divides into two paths and rejoins.

d. Circuit 4 has a single-pole, single-throw knife switch for turning a bulb on and off.

e. Circuit 5 has a single-pole, double-throw knife switch that can be used to turn on one bulb or the other.

f. *Don't look at circuit 6 yet.* It's a fun one to try to design yourself: a two-location light switch with two single-pole, double-throw knife switches. Imagine a stairway with one light. From *two* locations (with a switch at each location), such as the upper floor and the lower floor, you can turn the bulb on if it's off, or off if it's on, regardless of the position of the other switch. After you've built this circuit, can you make a three-location switch?

2. Now you're ready to build, and test, other circuits of your own design.

References

Awesome Experiments in Electricity and Magnetism by Michael Dispezio (New York: Sterling, 2000).

Benjamin Franklin's Adventures with Electricity (Science Stories series) by Beverley Birch (Hauppauge, N.Y.: Barron's Juveniles, 1996).

Blinkers and Buzzers: Building and Experimenting with Electricity and Magnetism by Bernie Zubrowski (Topeka, Kans.: Econo-Clad Books, 1999).

Electricity and Magnetism (Making Science Work series) by Terry Jennings (Orlando, Fla.: Raintree/Steck Vaughn, 1998).

The Thomas Edison Book of Easy and Incredible Experiments by James G. Cook (New York: John Wiley & Sons, 1988).

41 Making an Electroscope

We've all experienced a shock at some point in the winter, when reaching for a doorknob after walking across a rug. Believe it or not, this shock means you experienced an electric discharge of thousands of volts! **Static electricity** builds up when materials rub against each other, such as the rubber soles of your shoes against the rug.

> Rub a balloon against your hair or a sweater, and stick it to the wall. It is held there by the force of static electricity.

Electrons (subatomic particles that have a negative charge) rub off from one material to the other, causing a buildup of charge. When you rub your shoes against the rug, electrons are transferred from the rug to your body, giving your body a negative charge. When you reach for the doorknob, the electrons jump from your hand to the knob, causing you to feel a shock. Static electricity can be hundreds of thousands, even millions, of volts.

> You can get a shock of half a million volts without harm in the winter just from electricity. How can you live after such a shock? It's amperage (current) that kills you, not voltage. Dangerous electric sources, such as a wall outlet or lightning—another form of static electricity—have high electric current.

An **electroscope** is a device that shows the presence of electric charge. It contains a delicate piece of metal foil that moves when electrons flow through the electroscope. You can build an electroscope to investigate the electric charges in various materials.

Materials

- metric ruler
- marker
- thin piece of aluminum sheet metal (Scrap aluminum siding works well for the walls of your electroscope. You can sand it down to the shiny bare metal if it is coated.)
- safety goggles
- tin snips
- coffee cup
- duct tape
- epoxy
- aluminum foil or steel wool
- drill and bits (*requires adult help*)
- cork or rubber stopper
- scissors
- gold leaf (from an art store), platinum lead (from an electronics store or science supplier), or aluminum foil (from a gum wrapper)
- two 8-by-12-cm pieces of Plexiglas
- Lucite and glass rods
- wool and polyester remnants

Procedure

To Make the Electroscope

1. Measure and mark with a marker on aluminum sheet metal the dimensions of the following parts.

   Use tin snips to cut the parts out.

   a. Two sides that measure 6 by 12 cm each.

   b. A base and a top that measure 8 by 6 cm each.

   c. A disk that measures 6 cm in diameter. (Hint: You can trace the bottom of a cup to make the outline of your disk.)

   d. A rod that measures 8 by 1 cm.

> Wear safety goggles with side shields when cutting, drilling, or otherwise working with metal.

2. Attach the sheet-metal rod perpendicular to the center of the metal disk, using duct tape and/or epoxy. Make sure they are in electrical contact— that is, bare metal of each piece should be touching.

> To make a good contact, you can use aluminum foil or a clump of steel wool at the junction between the rod and the disk.

3. Have an adult first drill a 1-cm hole in a cork, then drill or cut in the middle of the top piece of the electroscope a hole that is big enough to hold the cork firmly.

4. Pass the rod through the hole in the cork so that 3 cm of the rod sticks out above the cork and the remainder hangs below. The rod should fit snugly inside the cork. Fasten the rod to the cork with epoxy if it is too loose.

5. Cut a 2-cm-long strip of foil from gold leaf. Attach one end of the foil 2 cm from the free end of the rod, using a tiny drop of epoxy, so that the foil is hinged to the rod.

6. Assemble the electroscope, using the metal sides, base, and top, and two 8-by-12-cm pieces of Plexiglas. You can use epoxy and/or duct tape to hold all the sides together except the top. Use only tape on the top, in case you need to remove it for adjustments.

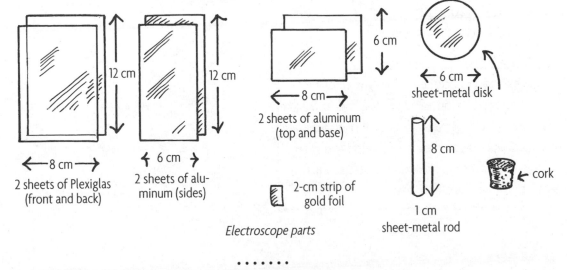

12 cm

2 sheets of Plexiglas (front and back)
←8 cm→

2 sheets of aluminum (sides)
6 cm

12 cm

2 sheets of aluminum (top and base)
←8 cm→

6 cm

sheet-metal disk
←6 cm→

8 cm

1 cm
sheet-metal rod

cork

2-cm strip of gold foil

Electroscope parts

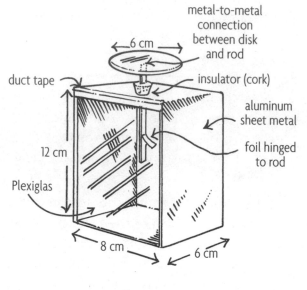

metal-to-metal
connection
between disk
and rod

← 6 cm →

duct tape

insulator (cork)

aluminum
sheet metal

12 cm

foil hinged
to rod

Plexiglas

← 8 cm →

← 6 cm →

Electroscope

To Test Your Electroscope

1. Rub a Lucite rod with a piece of wool to give it a negative charge. Bring it close to but not touching the disk on top of your electroscope. The foil in your electroscope should rise. Why? The negative charge of the Lucite **polarizes** the electroscope, separating the negative and positive charges. The negatively charged electrons are pushed down into the foil, which is then repelled by the similarly charged rod. When you pull the rod away, the foil should drop back down.

> What other material combinations would cause the electroscope to move? Try a glass rod with a polyester cloth. In general, electrical **insulators** are nonconductive, so they will develop and keep a charge better than **conductors,** materials such as metals that transmit electricity.

2. Rub the charged Lucite on the disk and pull the rod away. The foil remains elevated—you have given the whole disk-rod-foil apparatus a negative charge. When you touch the disk with your finger to ground it, the extra electrons go into your body, neutralizing the disk again.

3. Bring the rod close to but not touching the disk. Touch your finger to the disk for 2 seconds, then withdraw it. Now pull the rod away. The rod and foil should show evidence of a charge. This is an example of charging by **induction.** You used the rod to transmit a charge even though the rod never physically touched the electroscope.

References

Awesome Experiments in Electricity and Magnetism by Michael Dispezio (New York: Sterling, 2000).

Benjamin Franklin's Adventures with Electricity (Science Stories series) by Beverley Birch (Hauppauge, N.Y.: Barron's Juveniles, 1996).

Blinkers and Buzzers: Building and Experimenting with Electricity and Magnetism by Bernie Zubrowski (Topeka, Kans.: Econo-Clad Books, 1999).

42 Electric Pendulum

Pendulums have a variety of uses in machines and technology in general.

> A **pendulum** is a mass hanging from a fixed point by a string or other material that **oscillates** (swings) back and forth under the influence of gravity.

They keep the time in a cuckoo clock, they help ships navigate, and they can be used to measure acceleration. You can build a simple, inexpensive electric pendulum that will oscillate gently as long as you supply a weak electric current.

In 1851 within the dome of the Panthéon, the French physicist Jean-Bernard-Léon Foucault (1819–68) hung a 28-kg cannonball using 60 m of piano wire. On the floor, immediately below the cannonball, he sprinkled a layer of fine sand. A pointer fixed to the bottom of the ball traced in the sand, recording the movement of the pendulum. In order to keep the pendulum from wobbling, Foucault released the pendulum by burning a string that held it to one side. The pendulum made a true sweep, tracing a straight line in the sand. In a few minutes, the thin line had expanded into a pattern resembling the outline of a two-bladed propeller. The pattern grew in a clockwise direction, and at the end of an hour the line had turned 11 degrees. This could be explained only on the basis that Earth had turned on its axis beneath the pendulum, as predicted by Copernicus.

Materials
- 1 m of thin nylon fishing line (Two-kg-test monofilament works well.)
- 200-g mass

- metric ruler
- iron nut
- 2 clamps
- ring stand
- 4.5 to 6 m of insulated copper wire (Phone wire works well.)
- 10-by-0.5-cm iron bolt
- wire cutters
- 4-volt DC power supply (You can use flashlight/lantern batteries or an AC to DC converter available at RadioShack.)

Procedure

1. Tie one end of a nylon line to a mass. At a point 20 cm from the mass, pass the free end of the line through a nut twice so that the nut is secured in a loop when the line is taut. This will be your pendulum.

2. Tie the pendulum to a clamp and hang it on a stand to a length of 60 cm.

3. Make an electromagnet by winding insulated copper wire around an iron bolt. Leave 30 cm of wire free at each end, and leave 1 to 2 cm of the bolt exposed at each end. The more coils the better. You can go over the bolt with several layers—just make sure to keep winding in the same direction. Strip the insulation 1 to 2 cm from each end of the wire.

4. Use a right-angle clamp to clamp the bolt on the stand so that it is 1 to 2 cm away from and in line with the nut when the pendulum is still.

When electricity flows through a coil, it creates a magnetic field, through a process called electromagnetic induction. **Electromagnets** are used in electric bells, junkyards cranes, and security systems, to name just a few applications.

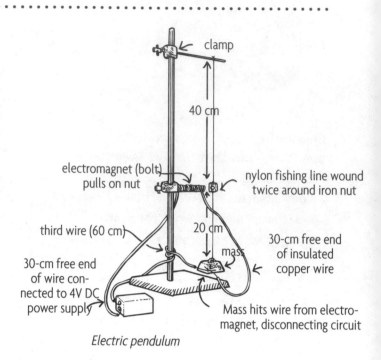

Electric pendulum

5. Attach one end of the copper wire from the electromagnet to one terminal of a 4-V DC power supply. Arrange the other end of the wire so that it gently rests near the edge of the pendulum.

6. Cut and prepare a third wire, approximately 60 cm in length. Attach one end to the free terminal of the power supply, then wrap the wire once or twice around the stand for support. Bend the wire so that the free end rests gently against the free end of the wire coming off the electromagnet. When the apparatus is constructed properly, the bare ends of the wires should touch each other gently until the mass swings into them.

7. Give the mass a gentle push toward the electromagnet. You may have to make some adjustments for the mass to keep swinging on its own. When adjusted properly, your pendulum will go through the following cycle:

Things you may want to adjust include the position of the wires, the positions of the nut and bolt, the length of the wires and number of coils, and the amount of electricity supplied to the electromagnet. (Do not exceed 6 to 8 V.)

a. The electromagnet, powered by a complete circuit, pulls on the nut.

b. This moves the pendulum toward the electromagnet.

c. The mass hits the wire from the electromagnet, causing the circuit to disconnect, consequently ending the magnetic attraction.

d. The pendulum swings back again, the wires touch again, and the cycle starts anew.

8. For a real challenge, try to build a working **Foucault pendulum.** Then try to build a navigational pendulum that maintains its plane of orientation even when you rotate the cart upon which it rests.

Ships, planes, and submarines all employ forms of navigational pendulums. These devices help the pilot determine direction and maintain a course.

Glossary

adhesion The attractive force between molecules of different substances.

aerodynamics The study of airflow across surfaces.

airfoils Structures such as airplane wings or propellers designed to provide force when air rushes past them.

algae Aquatic, plantlike organisms

amoeba (plural **amoebae**) A single-celled organism.

amp (ampere) A unit of electric current.

analytical chemistry A branch of chemistry concerned with the separation and composition of matter.

anemometer An instrument that measures wind speed.

angle of incidence The angle at which light strikes a surface.

angle of reflection The angle at which light reflects off a surface.

angstrom A tiny unit of length equal to one ten-billionth of a meter.

angular momentum A quantity based upon an object's mass and rate of rotation.

aperture (or **f-stop**) The size of the opening in a camera that lets in light.

astrolabe A device for determining the size and position of celestial bodies and other objects in the sky.

Bernoulli's principle The concept that as the speed of a liquid or gas increases, its pressure decreases.

binocular vision The ability to see with two eyes and determine depth.

bloom To become densely populated with microorganisms.

bridle In a kite, a span of string attached to the spline and spar.

buoyancy An upward force exerted on an object by its surrounding medium (liquid or gas).

calibrate To adjust a measuring instrument to read accurately.

capillary action The process by which liquids are drawn into narrow tubes.

carnivore A plant or animal that eats meat.

cast Something that is formed by putting a mold in a substance that is hardened to replicate the original object contained within the mold.

chemistry The study of matter.

chromatogram An image produced on paper in the process of chromatography.

chromatography An important technique in analytical chemistry for separating colored substances into individual pigments.

chrysalis The pupal stage of a butterfly and its protective covering.

cirrus clouds High, white, and wispy concentrations of atmospheric water vapor that precede light precipitation and fog.

cleavage The tendency of a mineral to break in the direction of its crystal system.

cocoon The silk casing around an insect during the pupal stage of its development.

cohesion The attraction between molecules of the same substance, such as soap solution to itself.

color addition The mixing of colored light rays, as in two theater lights whose beams overlap on a stage.

color subtraction The filtering out of colored light rays, as in white light passing through

two successive theater gels, or as in mixing paint.

compound A substance formed by chemically joining atoms of two or more elements in definite whole-number ratios.

compression The fossil remains of an organism within surrounding sediment.

concave Curved inward.

concentrated Being a solution to which a great amount of solute has been added.

condense To change from a vapor to a liquid.

conductor A substance or object that allows the passage of heat or electricity.

control A factor that is held constant during experimentation.

converge To come together at a focal point.

convex Curved outward.

Coriolis effect The observed effect of the Coriolis force.

Coriolis force An apparent force arising from the rotation of Earth that causes eddies in the atmosphere and thus affects weather patterns.

crystal The solid form of an element, chemical, or mixture, with a regular and repeating atomic structure.

crystal system One of six underlying structures of crystal forms—cubic, tetragonal, hexagonal, orthorhombic, monoclinic, and triclinic.

cumulonimbus clouds Large black concentrations of atmospheric water vapor that often lead to lightning, thunder, and heavy rain.

cumulus clouds White, fluffy-looking concentrations of atmospheric water vapor that usually accompany fair weather.

data Information gathered for scientific purposes.

density The ratio of mass to volume of a substance.

depth perception The ability to calculate distance through stereoscopic vision.

diffract To change the direction and intensity of waves by passing them by an obstacle or through a small opening.

diffraction pattern Regions of light and dark created when a light beam is passed through a slit filter.

dissipate To disperse or move away from a source.

diverge To move away from a focal point.

drag A frictional force in aerodynamics that slows down an object as it moves through liquids or gases.

eccentricity The deviation of an ellipse (such as Earth's orbit) from a perfect circle.

ectotherm A cold-blooded animal, whose body temperature varies with the surroundings.

elastic Able to stretch and contract.

electromagnet A magnet created by coiling insulated wire around an iron core and passing a current through the coil.

electron A subatomic particle that has a negative charge.

electroscope A device that is used to determine the presence of electric charge.

elements Substances that contain atoms with the same number of protons.

ellipse A curve generated by a point moving in such a way that the sum of the point's distances from two fixed points is a constant, as with planetary motion.

endotherm A warm-blooded animal, which maintains a constant body temperature.

eutrophication The decay of an aquatic system due to the depletion of oxygen and subsequent algal blooms.

evaporate To change from a liquid to a vapor.

experimentation The process of gathering, presenting, and interpreting data under controlled conditions following the scientific method.

filter To block out certain components of light or flowing matter while allowing others to pass through, as in color subtraction.

focal point A point of convergence of light rays bent by a convex lens or a parabolic mirror.

footcandle A unit of light intensity.

Foucault pendulum A long, heavy pendulum on a frictionless bearing that demonstrates the rotation of Earth through the pendulum's apparently shifting plane of motion.

f-stop See **aperture**.

fungus A group of plantlike organisms that consume dead and decaying matter.

genetics The study of inheritance of traits.

geothermal Pertaining to heat energy supplied by Earth.

glide ratio The rate of descent of a plane.

gnomon The part of a sundial that casts a shadow.

goniometer An instrument that measures angles.

gravity A weak mutual force of attraction between all matter.

heat engine A machine that transforms heat into mechanical energy.

heliocentric Sun-centered, as in the belief that the Sun is at the center of the solar system.

herbivore An animal that eats plants.

histology The study of organic tissues.

hormone A chemical substance that stimulates growth or other chemical activity.

hydrodynamics The study of the flow of water across surfaces.

hydrometer A device that measures either the density or the specific gravity of a liquid.

hydroponics The science of growing plants in nutrient solutions.

hygrometer A device that measures humidity.

hypothesis A possible explanation for a scientific problem.

igneous rocks Rocks produced when molten magma reaches the surface through volcanoes, flows as lava, and cools.

impressions Images left by plant or animal remains after they have been pressed against sediment such as clay or soil.

induction The process of giving something an electric charge by bringing a charged object close to it.

inert Unreactive (as with certain chemicals).

infrared radiation The portion of the electromagnetic spectrum that produces heat.

insectivore An animal that eats moths, flies, beetles, grubs, grasshoppers, and other insects.

insulator A substance or object that does not conduct heat or electricity.

interference A wave pattern that results when one wave overlaps another. **Constructive interference** occurs when the overlapping waves are in phase. **Destructive interference** occurs when the overlapping waves are out of phase.

ionic solid A substance that arises when two or more elements react to form a fixed crystalline structure.

larva A preliminary stage in the development of an insect.

latitude Distance north or south of the equator, measured by imaginary lines running east to west parallel to the equator.

lift An upward force that results from greater air pressure below an airfoil or wing than above it.

longitude Distance east or west of the prime meridian, measured by imaginary lines running from North Pole to South Pole.

lumen A unit of light intensity.

lunar eclipse A celestial event in which Earth passes between the Moon and the Sun, casting a partial or full shadow on the Moon.

magma Molten rock beneath the surface of Earth.

mass A measure of matter.

medium A surrounding substance; also a substance through which something else, such as a wave, travels.

metamorphic rocks Rocks altered by heat and pressure deep in Earth's crust.

meteors Fragments of matter from space that enter Earth's atmosphere and ignite from friction against atmospheric gases.

migrate In chemistry, to move into a surrounding medium.

minerals Chemical elements and compounds that occur naturally as products of inorganic processes.

Mohs' scale A mineral hardness scale ranging from 1 to 10 according to which any mineral can be scratched by a mineral of greater hardness.

mold Something that is made by surrounding plaster or other hardening material around an object.

molecular weight The sum of the protons and neutrons in an atom.

monolayer A layer one molecule thick.

nectar Sweet liquid produced by flowers to attract pollinating insects and animals.

nimbus clouds Low, dark concentrations of atmospheric water vapor that lead to rain or snow.

noble gas A substance having physical properties in between those of a solid and a liquid.

non-Newtonian fluid A substance having physical properties in between those of a solid and a liquid.

nutrients Chemicals that provide energy and promote or stimulate growth and life in plants and animals.

omnivore An animal that eats plants and meat.

optical interference A combination of light waves often resulting in the appearance of lines or colors.

optics The study of the refraction and reflection of light.

oscillate To swing steadily back and forth.

parabola A curve generated by a point moving in such a way that the point's distance from a fixed line is equal to its distance from a fixed point not on the line, as when the eccentricity of a planets orbit equals 1.

parallel circuit A circuit in which the components are arranged so that the electric current divides into two or more paths and rejoins.

payload The cargo on an aircraft or rocket.

peak The high point of a wave.

pendulum A mass hanging from a fixed point by a string or other material that oscillates

back and forth under the influence of gravity.

periscope An optical device for seeing above or below surfaces, or around corners.

phase One of three forms of matter—solid, liquid, or gas. Also the position of a peak or a trough of a wave.

phase change A change from one phase of matter to another through the transfer of heat.

phosphorescence The process by which a substance absorbs electromagnetic radiation at one wavelength and then releases it over time at another, as do glow-in-the-dark materials.

pigments Substances that impart color to materials.

polar Having a pair of charges that are equal and opposite.

polarize To separate positive and negative charges in an object.

polymers Long molecular chains.

precession The wobbling of Earth's axis over time.

precipitate To separate from a solution.

precipitation The process by which water vapor in the atmosphere condenses and falls to Earth's surface as ice crystals or liquid droplets.

pressure Force per unit area.

primary colors Pure colors of light(red, blue, and green) or pigment (red, yellow, and blue).

protoplasm The contents of the nucleus of a living cell.

pupa A life stage of an insect following the larval stage.

radial velocity The speed at which something turns in respect to angle.

reflect To bounce waves such as light rays off a surface.

refract To bend and change the velocity of waves entering a medium of different density.

regelation The melting and subsequent freezing of a solid due to the application and release of pressure.

relative humidity A measure of the amount of water in the air, as compared to the greatest possible amount that the air could hold at that temperature.

rocks Mixtures of minerals blended and bonded by ancient geological processes.

rotational velocity The speed and direction in which something turns.

salt A crystalline solid produced by the reaction of an acid with a base.

saturated A solution in which no more solute will dissolve.

scientific method The systematic way in which researchers pose and answer questions through experimentation.

secondary colors In light, colors produced by mixing two primary colors—cyan (green light plus blue light), magenta (red plus blue), and yellow (red plus green).

sedimentary rocks Rocks formed from the buildup of sediments deposited on riverbeds and ocean floors.

series circuit A circuit in which the components are arranged so that the electric current passes successively through each component.

shutter speed The length of time a camera shutter opens to permit the entry of light.

slime mold A primitive organism that resembles both an amoeba and a fungus, but does not fit neatly into the categories of animal, vegetable, or mineral.

sling psychrometer A device that compares the temperature of a wet-bulb thermometer with that of a dry-bulb thermometer for the purpose of determining relative humidity.

Snell's law A physics law which states that the angle of incidence is equal to the angle of reflection (of waves and light).

solar eclipse A celestial event in which the Moon passes between the Sun and Earth, casting a shadow on Earth.

soluble Able to dissolve in liquid. **Solutes** dissolve in **solvents,** forming a **solution.**

spar The horizontal member of a kite frame.

specific gravity The ratio of the density of a substance to the density of water weighed in air.

spline The vertical member of a kite frame.

sporangia A structure that produces spores.

spore A seedlike reproductive unit of plants.

static electricity The buildup of charge when one material rubs against another, such as the rubber soles of shoes against a rug.

stereoscopic vision The ability to see with two eyes, allowing depth perception.

stratus clouds Gray, low-lying concentrations of atmospheric water vapor that occur in layers and precede light precipitation and fog.

streak The color left by a mineral rubbed against a streak plate.

supersaturated A solution in which the solutes remain dissolved beyond the quantity that would ordinarily dissolve as the solution cools.

surface tension The contraction of the surface of a liquid arising from an imbalance of cohesive forces at or near the surface.

synchronous satellite An object that orbits a body at a matching rate, such as one that remains at the same point above Earth's surface.

tangential Touching but not intersecting a circle at one point on the circumference.

taxonomy The study of animal and plant classification.

thermal A rising body of warm air.

trace fossils Imprints of plants and creatures on surrounding material.

traits Features of an organism, such as hair color.

trough The low point of a wave.

turbulence An eddying movement of air masses.

unit cell The fundamental building block of something, such as a collection of molecules that repeats in a crystal.

variable A factor that is changed in the course of an experiment to examine its effects.

velocity Speed and direction; the rate of travel per unit time.

vernal equinox The equinox occurring in late March.

visible radiation The portion of the electromagnetic spectrum that produces light.

volt A unit of electrical potential difference and electromotive force.

vortex (plural **vortices**) A whirlpool of liquid or gas flowing about an axis.

wave A form of energy derived from the periodic motion of a solid, liquid, or gas.

wind tunnel A device that is used to study the aerodynamics of objects.

zenith The highest point in the sky.

Sources

The experiments and activities in this book are based on those originally published in the "Amateur Scientist" columns as they appeared in *Scientific American*.

**"Amateur Scientist" Columns
by Albert G. Ingalls**

"About a Hygrometer" (May 1954).

"About a Small Wind Tunnel" (April 1953).

"About Cultivating Algae from the Soil" (December 1954).

"About Historic and Modern Machines for the Generation of Static Electricity" (April 1955).

"About Home-Made Cloud Chambers" (September 1952).

"About Little Computers That Solve Puzzles" (March 1955).

"About the Pleasures of Paleontology" (January 1954).

"About Sundials" (September 1953).

"The Amateur Scientist" (May 1956).

"Mainly about a Theory of Color Harmony" (November 1953).

"Making a Cloud Chamber" (April 1953).

"The Making of Simple Mathematical Machines" (May 1953).

"On Collecting of Moths and Butterflies" (October 1954).

"On Culture of Plants without Soil" (October 1952).

"The Pleasures and Pitfalls of Archaeology" (July 1952).

"The Study of Rocks" (November 1952).

"Testing Airplanes in the Bathtub" (April 1954).

**"Amateur Scientist" Columns
by C. L. Stong**

"An Amateur Uses Paper Chromatography to Separate the Constituents of Mixtures" (July 1961).

"Apparatus to Demonstrate the Coriolis Force" (April 1960).

"Concerning Experiments with Rubber" (June 1960).

"Concerning Periscopes" (February 1961).

"Experiments with Wind: A Pendulum Anemometer" (October 1971).

"Growing Crystals Mimics Natural Mineralization" (October 1962).

"A Homemade Interferometer" (November 1956).

"How the Amateur Can Experiment with Films Only One Molecule Thick" (September 1961).

"How to Cultivate the Slime Molds and Perform Experiments on Them" (January 1966).

"How to Keep Various Reptiles Healthy and Happy in the Home" (July 1959).

"How to Make and Investigate Vortexes" (October 1963).

"How to Make a Pendulum" (June 1958).

"How to Make a Ripple Tank to Examine Wave Phenomena" (October 1962).

"How to Make a Series Interferometer" (June 1964).

"How to Measure Raindrops" (August 1965).

"How to Study Learning in the Sow Bug" (May 1969).

"The Lore and Aerodynamics of Making and Flying Kites" (April 1969).

"Mainly on Simulating Gravitational Fields with Droplets of Water on a Soap Bubble" (December 1964).

"Mostly about How to Study Artificial Satellites without Complex Equipment (January 1958).

"Mostly about Some Ingenious Ways of Studying the Artificial Satellites (October 1958).

"On Equipment to Study Freezing" (January 1968).

"On Experiments with Gibberellic Acid, Which Stimulates the Growth of Plants" (December 1958).

"On Reversing Cubes" (January 1965).

"A Sundial That Tells Clock Time" (March 1964).

"Two Amateurs Calculate the Exposure Needed to Photograph a Lunar Eclipse" (October 1960).

"Various Experiments for a Rainy Weekend" (April 1961).

"Various Kinds of Chromatography, Especially the Thin-Layer Method" (March 1969).

"A Young Amateur Experiments with a Plant That Collapses Its Leaves When It Is Touched" (March 1961).

We should also acknowledge Dr. Shawn Carlson, the current "Amateur Scientist" columnist, who was recently honored with the MacArthur Foundation "Genius" Grant for his contributions to science and education.

Index